HEALING BODY
MEDITATIONS

Also by Mike Annesley:
Practical Mindfulness (DK)

HEALING BODY MEDITATIONS

30 MANDALAS TO ENHANCE YOUR HEALTH AND WELL-BEING

Mike Annesley
with Steve Nobel

eddison
BOOKS LIMITED

This edition first published in Great Britain in 2018 by
Eddison Books Limited
St Chad's House, 148 King's Cross Road
London WC1X 9DH
www.eddisonbooks.com

British Library Cataloguing-in-Publication data available on request.

ISBN 978-1-85906-073-5

1 3 5 7 9 10 8 6 4 2

Typeset in Ehrhardt MT using InDesign on Apple Macintosh
Printed in China

PLEASE NOTE
The author, packager and publisher cannot accept any responsibility for
misadventure resulting from the practice of any of the principles and techniques
set out in this book. This book is not intended as guidance for the treatment of
serious health problems; please refer to a medical professional if you are in
any doubt about any aspect of your condition.

"Natural forces within us are the true healers of disease."
Hippocrates

"Healing comes only from that which leads the patient beyond
himself and beyond his entanglements with ego …"
Carl Jung

C O N T

E N T S

FOREWORD

The basic principle behind this innovative book of healing meditations is the transforming power of imagery – of symbols.

Why are symbols important? Well, as Carl Jung pointed out, they emerge from our highest aspirations and also from our deepest psychic roots. The prehistoric cave paintings of Lascaux, France, remind us that symbols have been with us since the dawn of civilization. In our modern world we are constantly surrounded by them. How many people would fail to recognize the Stars and Stripes flag or the bitten Apple on our iPhone or iPad? We do not always grasp, however, the far-reaching daily effect symbols and metaphors have on us. Their power to influence us has been long known to advertisers, which is why millions have been invested to find the right symbols to shape our buying habits. We find symbols, too, in global culture throughout history, and from there they have passed into our own minds.

In our complex inner lives, symbolism is an internal language whereby our unconscious minds attempt to communicate meaning to us. Many books have been written on interpreting dream symbology. What is not so often considered is that this symbolic language is a two-way street. This means that, just as our unconscious speaks to us, we can learn to speak back. Using symbols in this way can help to enrich many aspects of our lives. It can help to enhance our peace of mind and our vitality, and also generate healing – which is, of course, what this book is all about.

I was introduced to the incredible power of working with symbols in my early 30s when I began studying Wicca. This spiritual-magical path, among others, taught me the value and power of meditation. It also taught me how to use simple ritual and symbols for healing and personal empowerment. Quite quickly I learned that focusing on symbols has different effects on my psychological state. For instance, it is hard to feel depressed or upset while focusing on an image such as a field of golden sunflowers glowing in the midday sun. Similarly, I discovered symbols can be used to activate the resources of the unconscious mind. One powerful energizing practice I learned many years ago was to meditate on all the chakras, picturing them as different-coloured vibrant flowers opening from the base of spine to the crown of the head. This is a useful technique I continue to this day.

This book has very specific practices you can deploy to access the miraculous healing power of the body. I know from personal experience that this is more than just theory. Let me now give you one powerful example.

A few months before writing this foreword, a dramatic situation arose with Eva, my young granddaughter. She had half a finger amputated in an accident in the home and was rushed to hospital. The finger was surgically sewn back on. However, we were warned after the operation that there was only a 50 per cent chance it would "take". After a few days, we saw her finger was not healing properly: we were all concerned that it had an unhealthy black-blue hue. I spoke with her mother and was given permission to try a healing meditation with Eva. This meditation involved using "The Force" from *Star Wars*. I had introduced her to the whole series of *Star Wars* films a year or so before the accident and she absolutely loved them. I agreed with Eva to speak with her every day until her finger healed. Eva was amazing. She never once questioned the process. So, using this healing metaphor, I called her for about 10 days. We spoke on the phone or on Facetime, and I guided her to breathe in The Force through the crown chakra all the way down into the heart chakra, and from there into her hand and then down into her finger. I did the meditation with her and imagined I was healing also. As we did this, I described The Force as a bright healing light, and I also affirmed her natural ability to heal. Eva believed The Force could do many incredible things: she had seen it on TV a number of times. I worked with this belief, and very soon her finger was happily restored to a normal healthy colour!

This is just one example of the healing power of symbols. The visual dimension enhances that power for those who are visually inclined. Mandalas, which are potent healing diagrams charged with empowering symbolism, remind us of our relation to personal and universal forces that can be accessed through the language of resonant imagery. In this book you will find 30 beautiful mandalas with clear instructions to help you, the reader, address specific concerns and move towards greater health and well-being.

Bright blessings!

Steve Nobel

INTRODUCTION

The 30 mandala meditations in this book have been specially devised
to address the meditator's relationship with his or her own body, and with
symptoms such as pain, fatigue and anxiety. Hence they depart in imaginative
ways from traditional mandala patterns. However, the basic principles they follow
are long-established: the idea of using visual imagery for focusing the mind
through mindful awareness; and the increasingly known connections between
meditation and healing. This Introduction looks at such important contextual topics
as well as describing the chakras – since each chapter of the book begins
with a chakra mandala meditation. To conclude, there are helpful suggestions
about how to use the book most effectively.

MEDITATION AND MANDALAS

A few of the meditations in this book use mantras and affirmations.
But all 30 are based on the long-established tradition of mandala meditation,
using symbolic elements within a design to stimulate healing thought.

Meditation is a time-honoured mind and body practice widely used not only for spiritual self-development but also for enhancing calmness and physical relaxation, addressing psychological problems such as anxiety and stress, coping with illness and generally boosting health and well-being. There are many different ways to meditate, but most have four ingredients in common. First, it is usual to find a quiet and peaceful place with minimal distractions. Second, a relaxed, open frame of mind is taken as the starting point: distractions will inevitably enter the mind, but you let them go without engaging with them. Third, a particular posture is adopted: you might sit (cross-legged or otherwise), walk or lie down, but the position is consciously chosen. Lastly, meditating requires a focus of attention – something on which to concentrate the mind.

This is where mandalas come in. A mandala is a pictorial artwork or graphic design on which you meditate – often a painting, although ephemeral sand mandalas are a strand of the Tibetan tradition. The alternatives to using a mandala are to focus on a set of words or sounds (a mantra), or the sensation of your own breathing, or an object or phenomenon (such as a fruit or a candle flame), real or imagined.

The mandala was originally conceived as a symbolic image of the universe – an imaginary palace of the gods on which the practitioner meditates. Traditional Tibetan Buddhist mandalas feature a confusing array of deities, although in Hindu practice there was also a more geometrical kind of pattern, known as the Sri Yantra. The mandalas in this book are inspired more by the pictorial tradition than the abstract, although in some of the designs there are semi-abstract symbols, as well as naturalistic ones such as flowers and birds.

The popularity of mandalas in Western thinking regarding self-development is, to a certain extent, indebted to the work of the great Swiss psychoanalyst Carl Jung, who associated them

"Your vision will become clear only when you can look
into your own heart. Who looks outside, dreams;
who looks inside, awakes."

Carl Jung

THE SRI YANTRA
Originating in ancient India,
the Sri Yantra is an image of the
cosmos at the macro level and of
the human body at the micro level.
It consists of nine interlocking
triangles, surrounded by two rings
of lotus petals, with a central point
called the *bindu*. There is a gated
surround, known as the "earth
citadel". The downward-pointing
triangles symbolize Shakti, the
female principle, while the
upward-pointing ones denote
Shiva, the male principle.
The Sri Yantra maps a spiritual
pilgrimage in which every step
moves you away from limitation
and towards pure awareness.

with a harmonious, integrated personality. Inspired by Jung's example, mandalas came to be used as tools for inner exploration. The Jungian psychologist David Fontana put it well when he described how the symbolism of a mandala can help an individual "to access progressively deeper levels of the unconscious, ultimately assisting the meditator to experience a mystical sense of oneness with the ultimate unity from which the cosmos in all its manifold forms arises".

Such a sense of oneness can be achieved by the most profound kind of mandala meditation, which takes you into an awareness of the true nature of reality – an experience of pure being,

without any impingement from past or future, rational thought or troubling emotion. This kind of deep meditation, practised regularly, can make you more self-assured and resilient, more focused in your thinking, and more at ease with time, change and the ups and downs of fortune. By reducing stress, it can also make you less vulnerable to a whole range of illnesses and disorders (see pages 20–22).

Even less intense forms of meditation, in which the mind contemplates a variety of carefully chosen images and ideas, will be subtly beneficial, and in helping to relieve stress will reduce – to an unquantifiable degree – your susceptibility to many of the body's ills.

MINDFULNESS

Certain aspects of mindfulness are relevant to mandala meditation – for example,
the idea of letting go of irrelevant thoughts without judging yourself.
Some meditations in this book feature mindful interludes.

Many practitioners of medical science accept the validity of complementary approaches to healing. Herbalism is long established in both Chinese and Western cultures. Acupuncture has become commonplace in the West and may even be prescribed – or even occasionally practised – by orthodox health professionals. Another discipline, less commonly embraced by the medical establishment, is reiki, the art of healing by the laying on of hands.

Since the later 1990s "mindfulness meditation" has built up to its recent crescendo of popularity. Originally the idea that there is therapeutic or philosophical value in being in the moment, without worrying about past or future, and without judging any thoughts that pass through the mind, was an Eastern one. It began as a theme in Hindu yoga around 1500 BCE, and later featured in Buddhism (in focusing on breathing). In Buddhism, "correct" or "right mindfulness" is one of the precepts of the Noble Eightfold Path.

A landmark moment in the popularization of mindfulness was the publication in 1991 of *Full Catastrophe Living* by Jon Kabat-Zinn. This book described how stress, pain and illness could be addressed through mindfulness meditation. Kabat-Zinn had founded the Stress Reduction Clinic at the University of Massachusetts Medical School, and used an eight-week mindfulness meditation programme as a stress-busting technique with great success. This was the start of the mindfulness revolution that led in 2004 to the UK health organization NICE supporting a form of mindfulness meditation to reduce the likelihood that people with a history of depression might suffer from a relapse.

This book does not include mindfulness meditations, since they have no use for mandalas. However, certain mindfulness principles do play a part here, most notably the value of focusing intently on your own breathing, or in some of the 30 meditations on other sensations you might be experiencing. This is an aspect of being in the present, letting any distractions (especially any thoughts about past or future) drift away, without judging yourself for having them.

MINDFUL BREATHING: A MEDITATION

Here is a simple meditation that clarifies what is meant by mindfulness practice.
The key elements are:
being in the moment, letting any thoughts drift away without worrying about them,
and not making judgments of any kind.

1

Sit comfortably, upright but relaxed in a chair.

2

Notice your body. Attend to all the sensations you experience, however small.

3

Focus your attention on your breathing. Notice where you feel it in your body.
Tune into a part of your body where you feel your breath distinctly –
perhaps the rise and fall of the lower abdomen or air entering
and leaving the nostrils.

4

If your mind wanders, don't judge yourself. Just be aware that you have lost
your focus and move it back to your breathing.

5

Continue this for five or more minutes.

THE CHAKRAS

The chakras, more complex than mindfulness, nevertheless have a vital role to play in healing meditation. They reflect a complete system for understanding energy flow in the body. By meditating on the chakras, you can correct imbalances that harm your health.

Another Eastern construct to enter Western practice is the chakra system – the seven centres in the body through which energy, or prana, flows. Energy in the chakras blocked by stress or by emotional or physical problems can often lead to illness; free-flowing energy, on the other hand, keeps us healthy, vibrant and alive. Energy flow may be eased by meditating deeply on one of the chakras.

The mandala meditations in this book have been organized around the seven chakras, partly to provide helpful thematic orientation points for the reader, partly to introduce some traditional mandalas among the ones specially devised by the author.

Chakra symbolism traditionally features the lotus flower, the importance of which – in Eastern thought – derives from an aspect of its habitat. Rooted in mud, yet beautifully flowering in air, the lotus represents our own capability for transcending the limitations of the flesh.

Just as the lotus's ambition is to lift itself towards the sun, so we too aspire to enlightenment, represented by the thousand-petalled lotus of the crown chakra.

Each chakra may be thought of as an antenna, which both transmits and receives energy, and at the same time as a point of intersection between your consciousness and your physical body. In Eastern thought it is a fallacy to imagine that inner and outer selves are separate: they are in fact deeply interrelated parts of a harmonious whole. Lifestyle, morality, health and well-being are different aspects of the same totality.

Chakra meditation is potentially life-enhancing, and anyone interested in the subject would do well to consult a specialized book such as Swami Saradananda's *Chakra Meditation*. The chakra mandalas given here, intended as a painless introduction to a fascinating subject, should be approached in a spirit of adventurous experiment.

"Most powerful is he who has himself in his own power."

Seneca

THE SEVEN CHAKRAS

In the Indian healing tradition chakras are the seven energy centres progressing from the base of the spine to the crown. By meditating to rebalance out-of-alignment chakras you enhance your well-being.

Crown chakra
pages 142–145

Third eye chakra
pages 120–123

Throat chakra
pages 102–105

Heart chakra
pages 84–87

Solar plexus chakra
pages 66–69

Sacral chakra
pages 44–47

Root chakra
pages 26–29

The chakras are thought of as swirling wheels of energy corresponding to important nerve centres in the body. The energy flows through them, but may become blocked.

Each of the chakras relates to particular organs, body systems and states of being.
See the individual chakra mandala meditations on the pages noted in italics (above right).

MEDITATION BASICS

Meditation is simply a purposeful version of what many of us do quite naturally all the time – become lost in thought. It can put us back in charge of our own lives, with implications for those who suffer pain or are anxious about illness.

When beginners go wrong and give up on meditation, this is often because they find it daunting. They may be unable to concentrate, perhaps because they are too self-conscious about the possibility that they are doing it incorrectly. Or they find they remain unchanged during the experience, despite their expectations of transformation, and this bothers them. In fact, however, meditation is quite simple, and is best treated as such. The practice is certainly life-changing, but you won't notice significant changes during any single session.

After doing the mindfulness breathing meditation on page 15, a good way to progress is to try meditating on a candle flame. Go through the preparatory stages described opposite (first three points in *Practical guidelines*) and, when you feel ready, gaze softly at the flame. Allow your mind to quieten as you do so. Your intention is to focus on the flame, and nothing else. However, you will inevitably find that thoughts enter your mind unbidden. Whenever this happens, think of them, if it helps, as clouds that you simply let drift away, out of the clear sky of your focusing mind. Do not engage with any thoughts and do not actively resist them. Do not push them away, as this is a form of engagement. Just allow them to drift away as you return your attention to the candle flame.

Do not be concerned if your mind stays busy, and don't judge yourself if you find it difficult to focus on the flame. Just keep gently meditating – it still counts as meditating even if your mind keeps wandering and you have to keep bringing it back to your point of focus: you are not failing.

To conclude the meditation, gently take your focus away from the flame and return your attention to the room you are in. It is common to give thanks after a meditation, for the opportunity you have had to perform it, but this is not essential.

"To be in harmony with the wholeness of things is to not have anxiety over our imperfections."

Dogen Zenji

PRACTICAL GUIDELINES

Here are some guidelines to help those who are new to meditation. Be sure, also, that you don't lapse into any of the common fallacies – for example, the idea that meditation is only for spiritual people, that it is a kind of self-hypnosis, that you need to have inner calm to do it properly, or that it involves emptying your mind.

SETTING / SITTING

Find somewhere quiet where you won't be disturbed for 15 minutes or more. You don't need to sit in the lotus position. Just sit on a chair with your feet on the ground, relax and rest your hands on your lap. If you like, you can sit cross-legged on the floor using a meditation cushion for support. Note that you should not force your back into an unnatural position, nor should you slouch: let your back keep its natural curve.

BREATHING

The basic rule is to breathe naturally, with slow and deep breaths. Inhale with your nose, exhale from your mouth. You may take as long as you wish to get the rhythm of your breathing right before you start.

TIMING

You don't have to be prescriptive with yourself about how long you spend meditating. However, you might find you keep being distracted by thoughts such as: Am I halfway through? Is it time to stop yet? In this case, it might help to use the timer on your mobile phone, or you could use an online meditation timer.

AWARENESS

Once you have started to breathe slowly, you will start to feel more relaxed. When you reach this state, start focusing on your breaths one by one for a few minutes, before you start the meditation proper. If your attention wanders, don't be concerned: just bring it gently back to your breathing.

BENEFITS OF MEDITATION

The goal of meditation is not to relax, but simply to be, in the present moment. Relaxation, however, is often a valued outcome of the practice.

Through meditation we find ourselves more able to accept things as they are, to make positive decisions about our health and well-being, and to deal with anxiety about past, present and future alike.

Studies on the effects of meditation on the individual practitioner have noted the following physiological and mental benefits, even over a short period:

* Reduced blood pressure
* Improved blood circulation
* Reduced heart rate
* Slower breathing
* Reduced perspiration
* Reduced anxiety
* Reduced stress
* Deeper relaxation
* Heightened well-being

HOW MEDITATION CAN HEAL THE BODY

Scientific researchers are building up evidence to prove what meditation practitioners have long suspected: that, as well as having benefits for mind and spirit, meditation can reduce symptoms of the body's ailments.

Meditation is both focusing and pacifying. It is a time-honoured way to settle our anxieties and fears. It does that not by offering us soothing comfort but by concentrating our mind upon essentials: the underlying "rightness" of our being here in the universe now. By opening our perceptions and giving due attention to the simple truth of being, it reconnects us to what really matters while allowing ephemeral worries – about status, work pressure, tensions within our relationships – to fade away.

Also, anyone who meditates is likely to find that physically they become more at ease, and it is through this peacefulness that the body starts to heal itself, throwing off the tensions, fatigues and toxins that have accumulated during everyday life. More specifically, key health benefits have been observed, including stress reduction, improved sleep, lower blood pressure, improved cardiovascular function and even improved immunity.

Dr Andrew Weill, among many other scientists, has traced the connections between stress – as a cause or exacerbating influence – and various manifestations of ill-health, such as heart disease, diabetes and asthma. By tackling stress we can limit the damage resulting from a range of different health problems. In one study, Professor Jon Kabat-Zinn, pioneer of mindfulness meditation, reported that the skin lesions of psoriasis patients who listened to meditation audio recordings cleared up four times faster than those who did no such practice. Other physiological benefits of meditation discovered include improved blood pressure levels, lower cholesterol, improved flow of air to the lungs, and significant slowing of the ageing process.

The connection between meditation and bodily health was known even in 17th-century Japan. A Zen master named Hakuin proposed that to cure a life-threatening illness the subject should place an imaginary ball of soft butter on their head and then vizualize it melting and flowing down the body. Such visualization techniques are now part of the repertoire used by those who base their healing therapies on the proven links between habitual meditation and optimized levels of well-being.

"The energy of the mind is the essence of life."

Aristotle

DIMENSIONS OF WELLNESS
Individual scientific research findings are seldom clear-cut in their conclusions, but in studies of the link between meditation and better health the mounting evidence tends to point one way. Here is a simplified diagram to show how the physical symptoms associated with four specific health problems can be reduced with regular meditation.

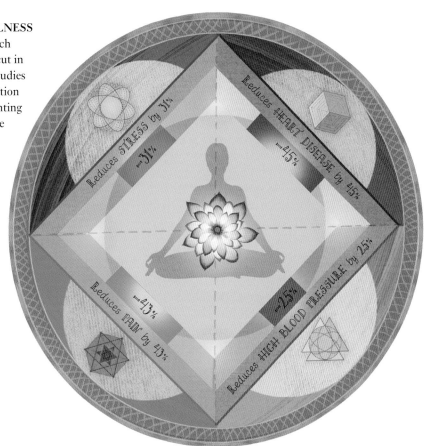

Reduces STRESS by 31% ~31%

Reduces HEART DISEASE by 45% ~45%

Reduces PAIN by 43% ~43%

Reduces HIGH BLOOD PRESSURE by 25% ~25%

QUICK-FIX IMMUNITY BOOST

The following simple meditation is designed to boost your inner strength when you are feeling unwell or off colour. Do it last thing at night, after getting into bed, as well as first thing in the morning, on waking.

1 Lie on your back and close your eyes. Select in turn a different part of your body on which to focus. Start with the feet and work your way up via the legs, abdomen and chest, to your arms and hands, and finally your head. Mentally tune into the energy of life flowing within each body part.

2 Imagine your life energy running within your whole body like an ocean wave, from your head to your toes and back again, twice.

3 Finally, hold in your mind a sense of your inner body in its wholeness, radiant with life energy. Savour the flooding of your whole body with healing consciousness.

HOW TO USE THIS BOOK

The mandalas in this book are meditation tools, to help you enhance your health and well-being. Apart from the specific benefits described for many of them, they are all intended to provide a positive foundation for healing.

These mandalas are far from traditional in their imagery: their unusual feature is that they are focused on particular body parts or systems. The idea is to encourage acceptance of the body and its processes. Often when we are ill, we shy away from our physical selves, and particularly the area that is troubling us. To engage in an accepting relationship with the fact of our illness, and with its symptoms, is to take one step towards summoning the resilience and adaptability that might enable us to live with the problem more comfortably.

Another principle behind this book is the idea that healing energy can be summoned by the mind and directed where needed by the power of the imagination. Expressed at its simplest, bringing positive, hopeful feelings to bear on a symptom or body part must be beneficial, since hope is the opposite of anxiety, and anxiety can make us feel worse and can even cause or exacerbate an illness. Hope, on the other hand, makes us stronger, in a better frame of mind to receive the body's natural healing and the work of health professionals.

Positive energy is also related to the power of intention, or the "law of attraction" as it is often called. By visualizing a goal, we can increase our chances of attaining it – an axiom followed by many sports and business people. Similarly, if you can visualize positive healing energy bathing, for example, a wound of some kind, and accelerating the healing, then the same principle of "attraction" or "intention" could be at work. In many of the meditations here the sun is seen as a reservoir of healing power, since it is literally the source of all energy in our solar system. At times, though, energy is visualized drawn up from the earth or taken from water or from some healing "elixir".

Energizing healing power *par excellence* is found in the Indian system of the seven chakras, which provides the structure for this book: each chapter is introduced with a chakra meditation. Before trying any of these, read about the chakras on page 16 and look at the chakra diagram there. If you are drawn to these chakra meditations, it is worth going deeper into the subject: look it up online or consult a specialized book.

It is intended that any of these mandala meditations will help you to make yourself resilient against illness or deal more positively with an illness you already have. Follow your intuitive judgment in selecting a particular mandala – it may not have an obvious connection with the body part or system you are concerned about, but there might be something in the imagery that draws you, or a phrase in the text. Some of the meditations include steps related to a specific medical issue – scan the text for these and modify them to fit your circumstances.

THE OPTIMUM APPROACH

*The following notes are intended to help you derive maximum benefit
from the mandalas and the accompanying meditations.*

REMEMBER THE STEPS

Make notes to help you remember the numbered steps when you are meditating on a mandala on the previous pages; or photocopy the steps for ease of use; or use the aide-memoire summary given for your convenience beneath each of the mandalas themselves.

BE OPEN-MINDED

Try not to undermine the effectiveness of a meditation by worrying about how it might help you. Just approach each one in a positive, trusting spirit. Monitoring the effectiveness of a meditation is a sure way to undermine its beneficial impact.

VALUE YOUR OWN POWERS

Bear in mind that it is not the mandalas themselves that are powerful: it is the healing energy of nature, whether derived from an external source (such as the sun) or from your own intrinsic vitality. Recognize and value this energy as you work with the mandala meditations.

REFLECT AND FOCUS

The meditations have relaxed, reflective steps as well as more focused kinds of thinking – for example, sometimes the meditation will end on a black dot rather than an image. Don't spend time worrying what is meant by words like "consider", "contemplate" or "relish". You are free to interpret such prescriptions as you wish: there is no right or wrong way to do these meditations. Don't worry where your reflections take you – but if you do find yourself wandering off the point during any particular step, just gently return your focus to the matter in hand.

MODIFY

Feel free to drop or change some of the steps if you prefer. You might even wish to devise your own meditation around a particular mandala. Bear in mind that the opening steps of a meditation are usually introductory: you can drop them if you wish after your initial acquaintance with a design, or alternatively you might prefer to follow the same steps every time if you enjoy them or find them stimulating.

"Health is a state of complete physical,
mental and social well-being, and not merely
the absence of disease or infirmity."

World Health Organization, 1948

CHAPTER 1

THE
FLOOR OF BEING

*Motion is key to our well-being. Keeping supple will involve some level
of exercise for as long as our bones, muscles and other body systems
allow us the power of movement. Yet stability is also essential – to stand
firm is to be strong, reliable, confident. As always, the literal meanings,
related to the body, shade metaphorically into the realm of virtues.
The mandala meditations in this chapter explore our relationship with
our bones and muscles, our legs and feet, with insights too into
values such as resilience and reflection.*

CHAKRA MEDITATION 1

THE ROOT CHAKRA

Sanskrit name: Muladhara

(literally meaning "root support")

Colour: Red

Element: Earth

Keywords: Stability, groundedness, shelter, sustenance

The root chakra, closest to earth, is the source of our stability and groundedness. Located at the base of the spine, in the coccyx, it plays a major part in survival and security – the simple fact of staying alive and being well enough to function. Linked with legs, feets, colon and (sometimes) adrenal glands, it controls the fight-or-flight response we show towards danger. When this chakra is open, we feel protected and confident, and optimistic about realizing our life's potential.

This chakra, in traditional yogic thinking, is where kundalini energy lies coiled: awakened by practice, this powerful energy rises to the crown chakra, to unify Shakti and Shiva – the feminine and masculine principles – in a process of psychic integration.

Meditating on the Root Chakra Mandala on the opposite page can facilitate the grounding of the self and give us the strength and determination to be healed when the body or mind is assaulted by illness.

Symptoms of a blocked root chakra may include insecurity, fear, defensiveness and procrastination – an unwillingness to commit to a course of action and follow it through.

SIGNS OF AN OVERACTIVE ROOT CHAKRA

Bladder problems; constipation; fatigue; irascibility; argumentativeness; impatience; feeling of being stuck

SIGNS OF AN UNDERACTIVE ROOT CHAKRA

Evasiveness; indecisiveness; fearfulness; paranoia; greed; eating disorders; insecurity; self-delusion

THE MANDALA'S KEY ELEMENTS ARE

Four lotus petals:
These represent the four functions of the psyche: mind, intellect, consciousness and ego

Inverted triangle:
The downward-pointing tip is the seed, from which consciousness expands in an upward progress

"Courage is never to let your actions be influenced by your fears."

Arthur Koestler

Sit comfortably and focus on your breathing / Enter a relaxed awareness / Gaze at the mandala: four lotus petals; square; triangle; glyph / Think of the lotus as the life force and the square as rootedness / Imagine red molten energy, drawn from earth to surround the chakra at the base of your spine / Visualize that strength expanding upwards inside you and flowering in wisdom / Feel your inner strength and security

ROOT CHAKRA MEDITATION

STRENGTHENING YOUR FOUNDATIONS

The root chakra meditation draws upon earth energy, envisaged as a red molten flow within the body. This powerful force is gathered at the base of your spine and grows upwards within yourself, blossoming in an unbeatable combination of four-square strength and wisdom.

1

Sit comfortably with the Root Chakra Mandala (shown on the previous page) in front of you.

2

Empty your conscious mind of all concerns and attend to the rise and fall of your breathing. Inhale and exhale slowly. Be aware of yourself becoming more relaxed with each in-breath and, with each out-breath, moving deeper into awareness.

3

Now turn your attention to the Root Chakra Mandala. Run your gaze over the mandala image, starting with the outer frame and working inwards. Contemplate the four petals, then within them the square and inverted triangle, and around the triangle the central glyph, which summarizes the chakra's essence: the primal life force. Think of the square as stability and the colour red as earth energy.

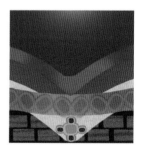

4

Contemplate the double symbolism of the mandala: the lotus representing the sacred essence of life emerging from the physical body, and the square meaning rootedness – the physical and spiritual aspects of the self firmly grounded in earth. Think, too, of the colour red as representing the primal life force.

5

Imagine the colour suffusing this chakra as red molten energy. Picture that energy as an infinite reservoir of power not only in your mind but also under your feet. With your mind, draw that power up into the root chakra at the base of your spine, where it rotates clockwise.

6

You have used the mandala as a portal to gain access to a tremendous fortifying and healing elixir. This will provide you with sustenance and self-confidence, combining physical with emotional strength. You know that you have the means to be secure and to let go of fear.

7

As your gaze penetrates the root chakra symbol at the heart of the mandala, imagine that the source of energy in your root chakra is not just power but also wisdom as it grows upwards, flowering into maturity. The inverted triangle within the mandala is acting as a map for your inner self-development. As your roots get stronger, the flower of the wise and mature self is able to grow strongly too – however bad the weather that buffets it.

8

Feel the molten energy of the root chakra filling your body and spirit, like the blood coursing through your blood vessels and capillaries. Remain for as long as you wish in this state of fortification: you are strong and the earth itself is your ally.

9

When you're ready, return your attention to the mandala on the page, using it as a bridge for your return to the everyday world.

"Fall seven times, stand up eight."

Japanese proverb

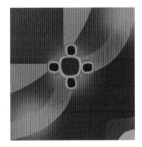

THE SKELETON AND MUSCLES: *THE SUPPLE BODY*

The skeleton gives us stability and protection, while the muscles give us movement, interpreting the commands of the brain. The intricate interplay of bone, muscle and mind is our wonderful daily dance on this Earth.

Together the skeleton and muscles make up the mechanics of the human form: the highly engineered, subtly articulated device that carries us from place to place and enables us to manipulate our environment.

We learn in later life what it means when mobility and dexterity are reduced. At the very least, we might struggle to climb a hill, or even the stairs, or to bend to tie a shoelace or dig for half an hour in the garden. Our joints might get inflamed and cause us pain, even at rest. Meditation, luckily, can have a powerful anti-inflammatory effect. One scientific study has shown that a group of people who did mindfulness training had lower levels of Interleukin 6, a biomarker of inflammation, than a control group who undertook less focused ways to relax. It is likely that stress reduction lies behind this finding, since stress is a known inflammation trigger.

The mandala opposite offers an exploration of the relationship between bone and muscle, with resonant symbolism. One of its aims is to liberate the skull (depicted as a dome) from associations with mortality, since the skull, after all, is nothing more macabre than a tough protection for the brain with all its connections – the inexhaustible wonder of consciousness. Also, the mandala brings us awareness of another natural miracle: the skeleton and muscles responding to the unvoiced commands we transmit through the nervous system.

This meditation helps us to relish the power of human agency: our ability to lift things, to travel, to be dextrous and to get things done, to labour for good purpose, and to express ourselves through movement. For those concerned about joint pain it provides a focus for sending anti-inflammatory energy where it is needed, by means of the healing solar rays.

The mandala also emphasizes, in the dome, the idea of the skull as a protective capstone. Both skull and dome are approximations of the half-sphere, a gesture towards the perfection and completeness of the globe. Our own skulls are robust though not indestructible vaults for the most precious wonder of all, conscious being, which is approachable through meditation but not, without falling into cliché, through words.

"The whole soul is in the whole body, in the bones and in the veins and in the heart ... "

Giordano Bruno

Focus on your breathing / Enter a relaxed awareness / Imagine yourself lifting the tree branch
in the forest – you are happy to tidy the clearing / Visualize warm, bright sunlight
penetrating your bones and muscles / Contemplate the dome – symbol of the protective skull /
Meditate on the tai chi symbols – a balance of yin and yang energy

SKELETON AND MUSCLES MEDITATION

TAKING ACTION

*In this practice, we start with a mindfulness audit of the body and progress
to a mandala meditation on the muscles moving the bones under the power of our
focused intention. All this takes place under the influence of the sun's energy,
whose anti-inflammatory powers are summoned.*

1

Sit comfortably with the Skeleton and Muscles Mandala (shown on the previous page) in front of you.

2

Empty your mind of thoughts and worries. Now concentrate on your breathing. Inhale and exhale slowly, becoming more relaxed with each in-breath and going deeper into awareness with each out-breath.

3

Before engaging with the mandala, pause for a few minutes of mindfulness. Starting with your toes, move your attention up each leg in turn, onto your body, and up each arm from the fingers, concluding with neck and head. During this exercise visualize your muscles and bones under the skin – the working parts of the engine that gives you power to do good things.

Now turn your attention to the mandala. Imagine yourself copying the figure, putting to use your muscles and bones, lifting heavy branches, chopping wood and tidying the forest clearing – this is the job you have to do.

There are certain tasks you lack the strength for, but where necessary you find workarounds – for example, chopping a branch in two before dragging along each half separately. You rejoice in all the movements of which you are capable. All this is work, not play, but you are happy to be of service.

You are working in summer sunlight, which blazes down from three suns charged with infinite healing energy. Pause for a minute or so in your imaginary work to contemplate the triple sun depicted in the mandala. As you gaze at the suns, spend a few minutes feeling the solar warmth penetrating your skin and strengthening your bones and muscles.

Be aware also, for a further couple of minutes, of that solar energy massaging all your joints, the ultimate anti-inflammatory agent of healing. You feel your whole body relax and become more supple as you meditate.

Finally, turn your gaze to the dome in the mandala. Recognize this as a metaphor for your skull. Just as your brain is protected by your skull, so too your essential being is protected by your positive spirit – your faith in the meaning and purpose of life.

Conclude by contemplating the tai chi symbols. Feel within yourself the perfect balance of energies they represent. Select any one of the points of light or dark within the symbols and take your mind through this portal into a profound awareness of being itself – the ultimate reality. Whenever you feel ready, return your thoughts to the everyday moment, feeling – paradoxically – deeply refreshed by your labours.

"Start by doing what's necessary; then do what's possible; and suddenly you are doing the impossible."

Francis of Assisi

THE LEGS:
RHYTHMS OF MOVEMENT

Walking, in the Zen tradition, can be a form of meditation (kinyin).
Another approach, more cerebral, is to make the legs, with their connotations
of adventure and connectedness, the focus of a mandala practice.

The leg allows us to approach each other, and can therefore be seen as a symbol of social bonding. A society characterized by healthy exchange – of trade, of resources, of ideas, of charity – is one where people move around freely.

Walking has obvious health benefits, for heart health, circulation, lung power, digestion, immune system and bone density, but equally important for spiritual well-being is the sense of self-sufficiency: look back and you will often be surprised at how far you have come.

One characteristic of walking is its natural rhythm, which, like a shaman's drumbeat, offers a parallel to the perpetual pulsing of the heart. There is an element of trust in this, since we do not make our strides one by one with conscious will, but instead we simply get the ambulatory process started, relying on our inner autopilot to continue it unconsciously.

Walking as a meditation, indoors or out, is a form of mindfulness: the idea is to walk very slowly and focus meditatively, within the moment, on the sensations in our muscles as we do so. At the more relaxed end of the spectrum is the "philosopher's walk" – a country amble that allows you, either alone or in dialogue with a companion, time and inspiration to range freely over philosophical issues and perhaps come to profound insights. The inspiration comes from nature – more specifically from pleasing views of a landscape or gardens. The archetypal Philosopher's Walk is a path that follows a tree-lined canal in Kyoto, but the feature has also been adopted by German university towns.

The mandala here encourages you to envisage healing, whether spiritual or physical, as a path, along which to travel in a natural rhythm. The journey towards well-being or fulfilment may be long and twisting, with some apparent backtracking. But the sense of ongoing practice – of putting one foot in front of another and moving forward, in a positive frame of mind, as encouraged by this meditation – is one that will suffuse the mind with purpose and hope. This is true regardless of whether you have an immobilizing condition. The journey, in any case, is not to be taken too literally, since inward travel, in mind and spirit, can accomplish far more than outward, into the everyday world.

"In the morning a man walks with his whole body;
in the evening, only with his legs."

Ralph Waldo Emerson

Focus on your breathing / Enter a relaxed awareness / Contemplate the walker and the path,
lake and mountains / Look at the bicycle border – another pace of travel / Imagine you are the walker,
with a journal for your best insights / Think of yourself resting by the lake and writing up new thoughts /
Walk on / Find deep rest in the refuge hut

LEGS MEDITATION

MOVING FORWARD

In this mandala meditation, we discover the rhythm of determined step-by-step progress.
The image shows a walker, but for those who lack mobility this may be interpreted
as moving forward in one's journey of self-development – for example, in dealing
with an illness or progressing with recuperation.

1

Sit comfortably with the Legs Mandala (shown on the previous page) in front of you.

2

Let all concerns and anxieties drift out of your consciousness. Be aware of the rise and fall of your breathing. Inhale and exhale slowly, becoming more and more relaxed with in-breath and going deeper into awareness with each out-breath.

3

Now turn your attention to the mandala. Contemplate the setting for the central walking figure. He walks around a lake – a place of mental refreshment. The path winds. There are mountains in the distance, with a refuge hut. Around the circular perimeter of the scene are bicycles – a reminder that different people are likely to progress at a different pace from yourself.

4

Gaze at the walking figure in the mandala, carrying a notebook. Imagine this is you. The notebook is a journal where you have written down the best thoughts you have had so far on your journey. After a while you stop by the lake to write up your latest thoughts.

5

Think of yourself hearing the lake water lapping on the shore, the breeze whispering in the trees and birdsong all around. Look at your surroundings too. As you rest, a precious thought comes to you out of the blue and you write it down in your journal: what is it?

6

As you get up and walk on, you become absorbed in the rhythm of your legs, doing your bidding without your overreaching yourself. You know that the important thing is not how far you travel but what you write in your book. Reflect on the experience or insight entered there.

7

Imagine your progress: soon you will be far away from where you are now. Look in the distance for the mountain hut, reached by steps. This is not the end of your journey, only a hospitable way station where you can spend the night.

8

Know that by the time you reach the hut you will have plenty of new thoughts to write up. You have met fellow travellers on the way. You are eager to write down their kind, wise words and what they have told you about their journey.

9

The entrance to the hut is intriguing: you cannot see what it will be like inside. Imagine progressing into the hut, which is full of rich insights others have left there, including the secret of inner peace: a sense of being fully at one with yourself and with the cosmos. As you walk across this threshold in your mind, a healing light floods your being.

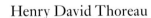

"I am alarmed when it happens that I have walked a mile into the woods bodily, without getting there in spirit."

Henry David Thoreau

THE FEET:
PILGRIM'S PROGRESS

Our feet give us direct and sustaining contact with earth, and are also the instrument of pilgrimage. Although tradition associates pilgrims with sandals, the bare foot, with its connotations of humility, makes a more telling symbol.

In a healing and spiritual context, the foot's most significant association is the pilgrimage, and by extension the idea of life itself as a journey. The pilgrim's progress through life is a linear path via innumerable challenges and occasional rewards. If the challenges are more numerous than the rewards, what sustains us is faith – for example, in the meaning of the quest, and the importance of doing en route whatever good we can, in a spirit of gratitude for all blessings received. One of these blessings is locomotion itself: our freedom to seek out places that offer the potential for fulfilment. Another is the incidental wonders, both human and natural, we are likely to encounter on the way.

If the foot has become a more resonant symbol than the leg for pilgrimage and other kinds of journey, that is because of its more compact shape as well as the fact that it makes direct contact with earth. The foot also leaves prints in soft earth, pointing to the importance of moral responsibility – one of the most obvious manifestations of this in the modern world being the "carbon footprint" left by CO_2 emissions. Going barefoot is a sign of moral maturity, reflecting natural simplicity rather than the material comfort offered by shoes: it is a form of sacrifice for the higher good.

Another symbolic dimension of the foot is the idea of being grounded – we might speak of both feet being firmly "planted". This metaphor in turn makes us think of the unshakable reliability of, say, the oak tree, in contrast to the more pliant bamboo of Eastern tradition. Legs and feet, it should be remembered, are crucial for standing still as much as for walking.

The mandala here explores these associations in the context of healing. Being grounded means being realistic – neither under- nor overstating the challenge faced. Oak-like resilience may be required: we will need to stand firm at times, resisting self-doubt or hopelessness. Something of the bamboo's flexibility may be needed too, to deal with change and avoid being stuck in negative thinking. Although being mentally steadfast and flexible simultaneously may seem like a contradiction, it is one that is consistent with human complexity. The mandala's complementary symbols reflect this complexity in a map by which to navigate towards the light.

"The foot feels the foot when it feels the ground."

Popular saying, mistakenly attributed to the Buddha

Focus on your breathing / Enter a relaxed awareness / Gaze at the washing of feet (trust) and
the oak (strength) / Think of love and care directed to washing your feet / Give thanks for healing love /
Contemplate the rooted strength of the oak / Visualize yourself as oak-like, and having the balance
implied by the four tai chi symbols

FEET MEDITATION

WASHING, STANDING, WALKING

This mandala meditation focuses on the washing of the feet, a resonant image of care,
also with implications related to supportive friendship, healing touch and selfless love.
Complementing this is an image of the strong, grounded self: the oak tree, whose
roots in the earth give resilience to the winds of change.

1

Sit comfortably with the Feet Mandala (depicted on the previous page) positioned in front of you.

2

Empty your mind of preoccupations and anxieties. Be aware of the rise and fall of your breathing. Inhale and exhale slowly, becoming more relaxed with each in-breath and going deeper into awareness with each out-breath.

3

Now turn your attention to the mandala. Gaze at the two major elements: the washing of the feet, symbolizing vulnerability and trust, and the oak tree, whose roots give it stability, self-reliance and strength in adversity. This balance of qualities – soft and hard, yielding and tough – is suggested, like all complementary balances in our lives, by the tai chi symbols, shown in footprint form at the four cardinal points of this mandala.

Contemplate first the washing of the feet in the bowl of water. Imagine feeling someone's touching, gently rubbing hands and the soothing warm water on your own actual feet: healing is coming both from nature and from human help. If you wish, imagine a particular person doing this service for you – a partner, family member, friend or nurse – and give grateful thanks for their selfless support.

You have placed yourself in someone's care, and this could be seen as a kind of vulnerability. But you know that from that vulnerability come strength and the ability and resolve to continue on your path. Feel that strength inside yourself and resolve to use it well.

Now turn your attention to the oak tree in the mandala. Now that your feet have been bathed and refreshed, think of yourself as being undaunted and imperturbable as that giant oak. Sense the oak growing inside you and filling you with resilience and wisdom.

You have enjoyed careful, sensitive treatment, motivated by love, and you are ready for whatever comes next. You might have a journey to make or a challenge wherever you find yourself. Your groundedness, like the oak tree's, will give you power to deal with any threats.

Feel powerful earth energy passing up into your feet, into your body and anchoring you as you continue this meditation. The earth and the mandala are working together, like a pair of healing hands, to fill you with natural courage and wisdom.

Contemplate the tai chi symbols, within foot-shaped profiles, and take inspiration from their complementary balance. You will have times of weakness as well as strength; your journey might go backwards as well as forwards; you will sometimes need to rest and sometimes be active in your healing. Conclude the meditation whenever you feel ready. Stand and take grounded steps, into new moments.

"Be sure you put your feet in the right place, then stand firm."

Abraham Lincoln

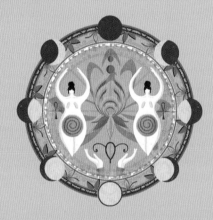

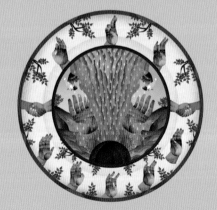

2

THE
CREATIVE BODY

Our most obvious creative function is the making of new human life –
which is not to say, of course, that this is a choice for everyone. This chapter
focuses on fertility and our relationship with our sexual organs, and on
the experience of pregnancy and the new-born. It also looks at creativity
in an everyday sense – the use of the hands to carry out our intentions and
to connect with others through touch. The Hands Mandala here
includes particular mudras (hand and finger gestures) with
numerous healing functions.

CHAKRA MEDITATION 2

THE SACRAL CHAKRA

Sanskrit name: Svadisthana

(literally meaning "sweetness" or "dwelling of the self")

Colour: Orange

Element: Water

Keywords: Feelings, sensuality, pleasure, creativity

The sacral chakra, centre of our feelings, emotions and pleasures, is responsible for our connection with others. It sits about 2 inches (5 centimetres) below the navel, in the lower abdomen, though it is also associated with the genital area.

This chakra gives us the richness of a life experienced through our feelings and through the five senses. Its energy allows us to move flexibly forward in self-development, relishing positive changes, with a full appreciation of the moment as we do so. Also, the sacral chakra is the source of everything we create – be it a garden, a drawing or a child in the womb.

Meditating on the Sacral Chakra Mandala opposite enables us more fully to appreciate our own well-being. It also deepens our experience of sensual pleasure, making intimacy more rewarding, and encourages us to be fluid in our responses to events and circumstances.

Imbalances in this chakra may result from the inhibitions imposed on us by society or by our upbringing, particularly in relation to sex and emotions.

SIGNS OF AN OVERACTIVE SACRAL CHAKRA

Issues in urinary or reproductive systems; heightened emotions; dependency on others; addictions; anxiety

SIGNS OF AN UNDERACTIVE SACRAL CHAKRA

Fear of pleasure; sluggishness; fatigue; low libido; negative thinking

THE MANDALA'S KEY ELEMENTS ARE

Six lotus petals

Moon crescent:

The upturned moon crescent represents the female cycle, the realm of subtle, non-assertive pleasures, the mystery of creativity and the changing nature of our feelings. Its upturned position suggests a bowl, which catches fleeting feelings like rain.

"Most people pursue pleasure with such breathless haste that they hurry past it."

Søren Kierkegaard

Sit comfortably and focus on your breathing / Enter a relaxed awareness / Gaze at the mandala: six lotus petals; upturned crescent moon; glyph / Think of the lotus as the spirit and the crescent moon as feelings, pleasure, mystery / Imagine orange energy filling the moon's bowl / Visualize orange power expanding inside you, activating the chakra / Feel your pleasures and relationships more intensely as you let go of guilt

SACRAL CHAKRA MEDITATION

CONNECTING WITH FEELINGS

In this mandala meditation, we concentrate above all on the crescent moon,
with its multi-layered symbolism. Focusing on this symbol, we awaken our feelings,
creativity and capacity for pleasure, and revitalize our relationships – which,
since love is a healing power, can steer us towards well-being.

1

Sit comfortably with the Sacral Chakra Mandala (shown on the previous page) in front of you.

2

Let all preoccupations and anxieties drift out of your conscious mind. Be aware of the rise and fall of your breathing. Inhale and exhale slowly, becoming more and more relaxed with in-breath and going deeper into awareness with each out-breath.

3

Now turn your relaxed attention to the mandala. Run your gaze over the main features of the mandala image, starting with the outer frame and working inwards. Contemplate the six petals, signifying the spirit, then within them the upturned crescent moon, providing a base for the chakra's main glyph, reaching up as if to surround the symbol in an embrace of awakened feelings. The moon signifies femininity.

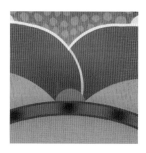

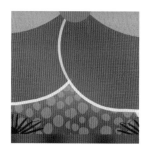

Think of the symbolism of the mandala: the lotus representing the spirit, which is capable, unlike the ego, of animating your feelings with goodness; and the crescent moon with all its complex associations of sensitivity, femininity, change, creativity, intimacy, pleasure and mystery. Let these ideas sit in your mind.

Contemplate also the colour orange, which is linked with strength and vitality. Then let all these associations dissolve in your mind and fill the crescent bowl of the moon, which you imagine filling up with the life force itself – like orange spring water.

Contemplate the crescent moon as a reflection of the life force – your creativity and your pleasure, which sometimes amount to the same thing, are indebted to your participation in a cosmos of infinite energy. They are your celebration of that energy, which fills your sacral chakra, in the pelvic area, with its sacred colour: orange.

Under the influence of the crescent moon, you feel a profound self-nurturing. Attend to your feelings: you are learning from them, so even mundane experiences are deepened into bliss. You are on the path of self-development, which will bring you the creativity to deal with any infirmities that befall you.

As your gaze penetrates the sacral symbol at the heart of the mandala, imagine its energy as an orange elixir pouring up through your feet and through your root chakra, then up into your lower abdomen below your navel. Visualize that energy as a force field swirling clockwise around your pelvis, spreading to the rest of your body in ripples.

Feel your sacral chakra opening like a flower – the six-petalled lotus in the mandala. You feel more in touch with yourself and with others. You let go of guilt and negativity. Your pleasures are more meaningful. Your relationships feel secure and rewarding – even deeply healing.

"We are going to the moon but that is not very far.
Man has so much farther to go within himself."

Anaïs Nin

MALE REPRODUCTIVE ORGANS:
SEED TIME

*Male sexuality has symbolic associations with abundance, hopefulness and
primal action, but such significance is always incomplete unless seen in the context
of female receptivity and, in the longer term, motherly nurture.*

A crudely dualistic view of the moral universe might place sex and spirituality at opposite poles from each other, but a more integrated outlook would bring them closer together.

The male organ of reproduction has attracted, with the help of popular feminism, an array of negative meanings that could be summarized by the phrase "patriarchal aggression". There are elements of acquisitiveness and exhibitionism here too: hence the idea of a sports car, for example, as a phallic symbol. However, in the context of healing, it is worth contemplating the more positive aspects of male sexual symbolism. Among these is the image of fecund emission: the shower of sperm that broadcasts its potency to facilitate a possible encounter with a single ovum. This can be seen as analogous to the miracle of life itself, created by a chance combination of biochemical factors in the mists of prehistory.

The male and female principles have been usefully distinguished throughout history as an interplay of the active and the receptive. Neither in itself has any effectiveness, which points to the importance of reciprocity, a harmonious balance of complementary energies. The most profound symbolic system underlying such a balance is the Chinese idea of yin and yang, which the mandala here incorporates.

Another concept embodied in this mandala is ambivalence. The endless knot which provides the basis of the image has both masculine and feminine aspects. The pointed ends of the triangle suggest a predominantly male function, but the central circle and the endlessness thread are characteristically female. The mandala, designed for both male and female practitioners, offers a holistic view of sexual generation, an experience of wholeness that is located in neither one gender nor the other.

This meditation serves a number of overlapping purposes. It is designed to address issues of sexual self-image, since both genders often need a confidence boost in this area of life; to encourage creativity, for which biological fertility is a profound metaphor; to celebrate the wonder of procreation and of the human existence generally; and to serve as a source of healing energy to help repair any wounds or malfunctions in the male genital area.

"Then is Love blessed, when from the cup of the body
he drinks the wine of the soul."

Richard Garnett, *De Flagello Myrteo*

Focus on your breathing / Enter a relaxed awareness / Gaze at the knot symbol (masculinity)
and beehive (fertility) / Trace the knot and visualize its power within yourself /
Contemplate beehive and flowers – the links between sustenance and fertility /
Gaze at the healing upper sun; and the tai chi suns, which rebalance your sex drive

MALE REPRODUCTIVE ORGANS MEDITATION

TUNING INTO MASCULINITY

The central image in this mandala meditation is a version of the ancient Celtic motif
of the endless knot, visualized as the source and biological function of maleness.
The meditation will help you deal with any self-esteem issues related to masculinity
(if you are a man) or trust issues (if you are a woman).

1

Sit comfortably with the Male Reproductive Organs Mandala (shown on the previous page) in front of you.

2

Take all preoccupations and worries away from your mind. Be conscious of the gentle rise and fall of your breathing. Inhale and exhale slowly, becoming more relaxed with each in-breath and going deeper into awareness with each out-breath.

3

Now turn your attention to the mandala. Contemplate the symbol of the endless knot. This is an emblem of masculinity – of yourself or else of your partner. Above is a beehive, seen as source of male fertility and self-expression. Flowers complete the picture, since bees (sperm) could not function without flowers (the other's organs). Be aware that these elements are within the self but do not constitute the self.

Gaze at the endless knot in the mandala, and trace its pathway. Think of this image as your emblem of masculinity. Visualize the knot in your genital area (or that of your partner) – mysterious and powerful. It lies within the self, full of potential, sometimes unruly. Any issues of self-esteem are in the mind, not in the organ.

Turn your attention to the beehive, imagining male fertility as a hive of bees which may or may not stray from their headquarters. They do not sting. Instead, they go about their business, visiting flowers for sustenance – the sustenance of intimacy. Think of the connections between sustenance and fertility.

Visualize a range of healthy foods being broken down in the stomach and then the nutrients passing into you. Bacteria in your gut are helping with the process. Together, a combination of nerves, hormones, bacteria, blood and the organs of the digestive system is completing the complex task of digestion.

Now let that solar energy fill your being, entering your eyes and pouring its healing, creative and fertile potency down into the male organs. You feel a sense of replenishment, of being recharged both physically and in terms of your self-esteem and self-confidence.

Turn your attention next to the tai chi suns at either side of the endless knot symbol. These represent yin and yang, female and male energies complementing each other and held in balance – in the male or female personality and in the cosmos. Feel a rebalancing within yourself: you are neither passive nor aggressive. Imagine these tai chi suns infiltrating the testicles, rebalancing your sexuality to make it more empathic to your partner.

Finally, gaze at the central dot in the endless knot. Enter it, as through a portal, into the mystery of fertility and creation, and indeed of life itself, whose inner core is simple, pure being, at the heart of all reproduction and all love.

"The sexual embrace can only be compared with music and with prayer."

Marcus Aurelius

FEMALE REPRODUCTIVE ORGANS: *THE FERTILE CRESCENT*

Abundance and generosity are qualities closely linked with the female reproductive organs – the vulva, vagina, ovaries and uterus (womb). They are rich in symbolism, suggestive in many traditions of the sacred mysteries.

Female fertility is symbolically linked with welcome, the admission of the Other into the porch of the self. The vulva relates to both ingress and egress: the admission of the male member, the offering of new life in its creative adventure. Whereas the male reproductive organ is a phenomenon of solar daylight, the female genitalia have traditionally been associated with lunar mysteries. In truth, of course, there is a wonderful mystery about both, especially in the sacred moment of their coming together.

The widespread idea of femininity as a healing energy derives from the woman's role as nurturer and also from her compassion, traditionally a female virtue, linked with the Mahayana Buddhist goddess Guanyin. If sex itself is seen by some as having potential healing power, there are three possible factors at work in this perception: first, it is healthy to inhabit the moment; second, touch and intimacy are therapeutically beneficial as expressions of love; and third, reproductive sex gives rise to healthy new life.

The mandala here makes use of the symbol of the flower-like cup or chalice, which relates not only to feminine receptiveness and abundance but also, via the Grail motif, to divinity. The cup, which has overtones of both the vulva and the breast, links the experienced moment and evolutionary purpose of coitus.

Since sexual fulfilment goes far beyond penetration and orgasm, the mandala takes a broader remit, gathering together resonant symbols to help to free the meditator (whether male or female) from sexual blocks, to encourage him or her to take pleasure in sexual contact of any description without measuring enjoyment according to conventional norms, and to celebrate sensual experience in general. It also aims to overcome any social conditioning that might have resulted in unhealthy inhibitions.

In addition, this mandala seeks to promote creativity, the artistic equivalent of procreation. It would be unrealistic, of course, to imagine that meditation on a mandala can increase physical fertility, but in providing a mirror of both the physical and inner self such practice may well be helpful as an orientation point in one's journey to come to terms with, or attempt to overcome, unwanted childlessness.

"The deepest experience of the creator is feminine, for it is experience of receiving and bearing."

Rainer Maria Rilke

Focus on your breathing / Enter a relaxed awareness / Gaze at the central image of femininity
and imagine it in your genitalia, charged with power / Draw upon the primal power of
the full-length women / Look at the moon's phases, linked with feelings / Bathe in moonlight
to refresh your emotions / Let the image of femininity fill you with peace

TUNING INTO FEMININITY

The central image here, based on a Celtic fertility symbol, is the flower-like cup,
sitting on leaves, suggesting the receptivity and benevolent giving of womanhood.
The women with the spiral of life in their bodies stand in a blessed sisterhood.
Beneath is a further fertility image, with protective hands of love.

1

Sit comfortably with the Female Reproductive Organs Mandala (shown on the previous page) in front of you.

2

Empty your mind of all concerns. Be aware of your breathing. Inhale and exhale slowly, becoming more relaxed with each in-breath and going deeper into awareness with each out-breath.

3

Now turn your attention to the mandala. Contemplate the central symbol of receptive fertility. This represents the feminine. Gaze also at the female organs, with protective hands around them, and the full-length sisters, with breasts and a spiral of sexual energy. Look, too, at the moon, in its phases, signifying menstruation and the feelings (see page 44, on the Sacral Chakra).

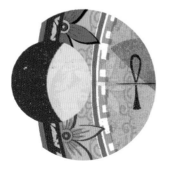  

4

Gaze at the central image of femininity and imagine it inside yourself, in your genital area (or that of your partner), charged with power. The circle suggests completeness, yet it is opening out with compassion. Are the two blue spheres being received or given? Are they the gifts of the fertile male or a more spiritual offering from a source you recognize or seek to find? In all its mystery the symbol inhabits the self, serene and full of promise.

5

Turn your attention to the two full-length women – the image is based on a pagan fertility carving. Think of your connection with the primal energy tapped by this prehistoric artwork. The eternal feminine is a universal archetype, saturated with mysterious power.

6

Gather this power into yourself as you meditate on the mandala. Imagine it as a source of healing and as a talisman that will promote fertility (if this is what you seek) or creativity.

7

Now gaze at the moon's phases. These are symbolic of the changes that shape your body and mind, while the spirit remains beyond them, invulnerable and unchanged. The moon connects you with your feelings. It transmits the life force in a reflected form more subtle and more enigmatic than direct energy pouring out from the sun.

8

Imagine yourself bathing in moonlight, balm for all past wounds in your life. Absorb this lovely light as emotional wisdom. Feel your relationships, with partner, family, friends, doctor, tingling now with a new vibrancy.

9

Return your attention to the central symbol. Do not interpret it this time. Simply let it sit in your mind, a reflection of what is most wise, powerful, mysterious and creative about your own self. Sit at peace in the knowledge that you can call up this symbol in your mind at any time, for any kind of reassurance you need.

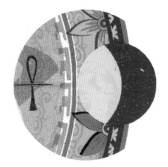

NEW LIFE:
MOTHER AND CHILD

Potentially, there is no more positive experience than bringing new life into the world.
Meditation for a mother is an excellent way to savour key stages in pregnancy
and connect healingly with the underlying natural miracle.

Pregnancy is a precious time of rapid change – in contrast to the usual mode by which time operates in the body, through scarcely perceptible ageing. To fully appreciate the natural miracle of new life in the womb, it helps to meditate mindfully, and the unborn child makes the perfect focus for such a practice, especially if he or she has already started to move within the belly.

There are many possible dimensions to such a meditation. The most obvious of these are: the wonder of growth and maternal sustenance, the innocence and purity of the embryo, the sense of immeasurable potential for a life not yet started, the unspoken communication between mother and child, and – above all – love, in a form both inexhaustibly giving and self-enriching. The mandala meditation here combines all these aspects and may be used at all stages of pregnancy, or after birth.

In symbolic terms, the mother connects with both earth and sea, since these, too, are wombs and wells of life. In a sense she has a sea inside herself: the amniotic fluid of the womb. The mother also serves a sheltering function, like a sea harbour or inlet.

Both mother and child are archetypes: images of universal power that are rooted in the unconscious, in all cultures, and appear frequently in dreams. To connect with such fundamental themes in a meditation is to participate in the elemental drama of life unfolding on Earth – the continuation of the species. This gives the practitioner a deep sense of cosmic connection. The mother, in carrying her child, is fulfilling a cosmic purpose. Reaching an awareness of this role in meditation can be deeply relaxing, putting incidental urges and anxieties into the shade.

Pregnancy in the modern age is monitored by the medical establishment, and this can undermine, at a subliminal level, the sense of carrying and delivering a child to the world as a privilege and gift of nature. The symbolic imagery of the mandala is designed to emphasize the naturalness of motherhood. Whatever the mother's spiritual beliefs, she can benefit from tuning into her own natural magic – the wisdom of the womb.

"The jewel of the sky is the sun,
the jewel of the house is the child."

Chinese saying

Focus on your breathing / Enter a relaxed awareness /
Meditate on the child in the womb – a kind of selfie / Attend to any sensations your baby causes /
Visualize the fluid in the womb as a healing elixir / Contemplate the child's potential /
Gaze on the harbour and think of your protective power / Imagine the child healing your hurts

NURTURING A MIRACLE

This meditation focuses on two stages of motherhood: pregnancy and nursing.
Though specifically intended for the mother-to-be, it may be used after birth,
as a reminder of a child's natural vitality and potential. Healing power is seen as
residing in the fluid of the womb and in the child herself / himself.

Sit comfortably with the New Life Mandala (shown on the previous page) in front of you.

Empty your mind of any worries or preoccupations. Focus lightly on your gentle breathing. Inhale and exhale slowly, becoming more and more relaxed with each in-breath and going deeper into awareness with each out-breath.

Contemplate the mandala. Gaze at the harbour wall – suggesting the mother's care and nurture. Look at new life in the womb, innocent and full of potential, and at two mothers nursing. As the mother, you have the ultimate privilege: of not only being the sacred courier for this package of body, mind and spirit, but also of shepherding it lovingly on its subsequent adventures.

Focus on the child in the womb depicted in the mandala, and think of this as a kind of selfie: a picture of the new person you are introducing to the world, who during pregnancy is still partly you. Visualize the child as both a new human being in the making and a maternal experience you are having in the moment. Spend a few minutes sharing quality time with him or her, living in the present.

If you can feel movement in your womb, attend to these sensations closely and joyfully (relinquish your contemplation of the mandala itself while doing this). Treat this part of your meditation as a mini-mindfulness practice.

Spend another few minutes visualizing your own amniotic fluid, in which the embryo floats, as an elixir bathing the baby in natural energy to strengthen its growing organs and body systems. Nature is nurture: you are drawing upon a natural force field to provide the healthiest start for your child.

There may be complications, but if so you have faith that under nature's care they will be resolved. Meanwhile you can rejoice in being a mother-to-be, one of the proudest roles anyone can fill in this life.

Gaze at one of the images of nursing, and think of this as a transmission of nurture in the broadest sense – including safety, shelter, food, education, moral values. Be at peace in the knowledge you will do your utmost to ensure your child is as happy and healthy as possible while under your care. You will be an exemplary mother and a loving playmate.

Imagine the sea inlet, with its harbour walls, as your loving embrace, protecting your child from storms. Your baby is a precious cargo in the ship of pregnancy. You are blessing him or her with well-being, but at the same time this healing influence is reciprocated: you are drawing healing power from the child inside you (or the child you are nursing).

"Mother's love grows by giving."
Charles Lamb

THE HANDS:
EXECUTIVE POWERS

The hand, being nimble, can be highly expressive. Four of the major functions associated with this body part – touch, craftsmanship, work and hand symbolism (mudras) – are rich sources of positive energy.

The hand symbolizes action and, by extension, authority and dominion – think of a hand signing a treaty or held up to halt a flow of traffic. For an even more resonant image, imagine a pianist watching his or her own hands so flawlessly playing a sonata that they seem to be scurrying creatures with a will of their own.

The dexterity of the hands in carrying the intentions of the mind can be astonishing. Craftsmanship can be pushed to uplifting virtuosity, as with the sculptor who renders the miracle of the body in a sublime work of bronze or marble. A mandala itself is a work of craftsmanship, whether painted, as in this book, or intricately assembled with coloured sands and used in meditation before being scattered back into nature, as in Tibetan Buddhist tradition.

There are two particular aspects of the hands' activity that flow into the stream of our well-being: touch and work. Touch is the native language of intimacy, more eloquent and healing than words. The energy that flows from a loved one's hands is all-powerful: it can cure, for example, a headache, since it carries the vital force of love to a clear point of focus. The handshake is a socialized version of intimate touch, suggesting that even strangers can share a flash of closeness.

Work is more ambivalent, but in its purest form, as manual labour, it presents us with one of the basic elements of the good life. Even if bed-bound, we can still do honest work in the surrogate form of a hand-focused meditation, such as the one linked to the mandala opposite, showing the washing of hands in a waterfall.

This mandala incorporates Buddhist mudras: traditional hand gestures and finger postures that convey benevolent intentions and can play a part in healing. The mudra of life increases vitality, enhances immunity and sharpens sight: you bend the ring finger and little finger (pinky) to touch the tip of the thumb, while leaving the other two fingers straight. The mudra of the sun relieves anxiety: you bend the ring finger and press its tip with the thumb. Another powerful mudra is the five-finger exercise by which the thumb touches each of the fingers in sequence, for a few seconds, starting with the index finger; in turn this fosters calm, patience, self-confidence and intuition.

"Often the hands will solve a mystery that the intellect has struggled with in vain."

Carl Jung

Focus on your breathing / Enter a relaxed awareness / Look at the mandala, including the mudras (therapeutic hand gestures) / Copy the mudras and five-finger exercise / Contemplate the doves being released from a pair of hands – your anxieties released / Think of your hands under total control / Vow to do something good with them soon

HEALING WITH NIMBLE FINGERS

In this practice, we explore the healing properties of hands. We invoke healing energy, by washing hands in a waterfall, to promote nimbleness in the joints and wrists. And we are introduced to the power of mudras – traditional Indian hand gestures, with healing properties.

1

Sit comfortably with the Hands Mandala (shown on the previous page) in front of you.

2

Empty your mind of any concerns you might have. Turn your relaxed attention to your breathing. Inhale and exhale slowly, becoming more and more relaxed with each in-breath and going deeper into awareness with each out-breath.

3

Gaze at the mandala with its pairs of hands and individual hands – a pair washing themselves under a waterfall, two handshakes, a pair releasing two doves, and hands in particular mudras (symbolic hand gestures in Buddhism and Hinduism). Think of the functions of hands: to pick things up or hold or move them, to touch and feel, to make signs, to perform a craft or art.

4

Returning your attention to the mandala, imagine washing your hands in a waterfall. Mime this action as you gaze at the image. Imagine the water as healing energy, lubricating your fingers and wrists.

5

Copy the mudras in the upper mandala border, spending a couple of minutes on each. Start with the mudra of knowledge: ring of index finger and thumb, the other fingers stretched out. This enhances brain and memory power. Then do the mudra of life: tips of little finger and ring finger touching thumb. This increases vitality. Then perform the mudra of the sun: ring finger bent and pressed by thumb. This reduces anxiety.

6

Do the five-finger exercise shown in the lower mandala border. Starting with the index finger, touch your thumb onto each of your fingers in turn for a few seconds. Do the sequence five times. This balances your energy.

7

Once you have finished the mudras and the five-finger exercise, contemplate the power of the hands. They are more than just functional tools. They convey love and respect through touch and can connect the rest of your body with healing energies.

8

Turn your attention back to the mandala and contemplate the doves being released from a pair of hands. As you gaze on this release and think about it happening, feel the release of all your anxieties. These perhaps made you wring your hands or tap your fingers nervously on a table. But now, as you let go of all fears, your hands enter your absolute control again. Feel the nimbleness flowing back into them.

9

End the meditation with an affirmation that you will do something useful and healing with your hands – perhaps a job for a neighbour, or writing a poem of thanksgiving, or giving your loved one a compassionate touch or healing massage.

"Without labour nothing prospers."

Sophocles

CHAPTER 3

THE
CENTRE OF BEING

Our sense of well-being comes primarily from the level of comfort we feel within our own skins, from having a clear and peaceful mind and from being able to perform everyday actions effectively. Central to well-being is freedom from anxiety, pain and fatigue. All three of these dimensions are the focus of a separate mandala meditation within this chapter. The chapter begins with a chakra mandala meditation based on the solar plexus, traditionally regarded as the core of the self.

CHAKRA MEDITATION 3

THE SOLAR PLEXUS CHAKRA

Sanskrit name: Manipura

(literally meaning "jewelled city")

Colour: Yellow

Element: Fire

Keywords: Will power, self-esteem, awareness, self-control

The solar plexus chakra is the core of who we are: our identity or personality. From this source our will power draws its strength.

Seated just above the navel and below the rib cage, this energy centre brings us confidence in our being and in our effectiveness within the world. It enables us to convert passivity into action, and to meet any challenges we may encounter on that journey of transformation. This is the chakra of being proactive rather than merely reactive.

Meditating on the Solar Plexus Chakra Mandala on the opposite page releases an awareness of empowerment in ourselves. We are confirmed in our conscious control over emotions and thoughts. We knowingly have power to choose – and this includes choosing healing rather than stagnation, actively seeking a cure for what can be cured, and living a life as full as possible, despite any condition deemed incurable.

Blockage of this chakra can cause mistrust of people in our lives and too much concern about how we are seen. When the chakra is in balance, we appreciate our own qualities and the unique contribution made by others to our mental, emotional and physical well-being.

SIGNS OF AN OVERACTIVE SOLAR PLEXUS CHAKRA

Harsh judgment of others; perfectionism; stubbornness; anger; aggressiveness; inability to compromise; being a workaholic

SIGNS OF AN UNDERACTIVE SOLAR PLEXUS CHAKRA

Doubting people; fear of solitude; anxiety; oversensitivity to others' opinions; reliance on others' approval

THE MANDALA'S KEY ELEMENTS ARE

Ten lotus petals
Inverted triangle:
The T-shaped projection on each of the three sides is a reference to the Hindu swastika, which is an ancient symbol for the sun. The sun is the empowering force of this chakra. Sometimes the triangle is depicted as red, to denote solar fire, but in many versions the T-shapes are not shown.

Sit comfortably and focus on your breathing / Enter a relaxed awareness /
Gaze at the mandala: ten lotus petals; triangle with T-shaped attachments; glyph /
Think of the lotus as the sacredness of life and the triangle as inner blossoming /
Imagine yellow solar energy, drawn from the sun to surround the chakra between navel and
rib cage / Visualize the "fire in your belly" / Feel your creative passion and will power

SOLAR PLEXUS CHAKRA MEDITATION

IGNITING YOUR INNER SUN

The solar plexus chakra meditation takes its strength from the sun – hence the yellow colouring of this mandala. By drawing solar energy into yourself, and activating the chakra, you can access creative passion and summon the will power to take transformative action and rise to any challenges.

1

Sit comfortably with the Solar Plexus Chakra Mandala (shown on previous page) in front of you.

2

Empty your conscious mind of worries and preoccupations and turn your attention to the rise and fall of your breathing. Inhale and exhale slowly. Be aware of yourself becoming more relaxed with each in-breath and, with each out-breath, moving deeper into awareness.

3

Now turn your relaxed attention to the mandala. Run your gaze over the main features of the mandala image, starting with the outer frame and working inwards. Contemplate the ten lotus petals, then within them the inverted triangle with its T-shaped append-ages (comprising an ancient sun symbol), and then the central glyph, which summarizes the chakra's essence: the core self, which is the source of our will power and action.

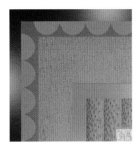

Think of the symbolism of the mandala: the lotus representing sacred life emerging out of the physical body, and the inverted triangle, meaning self-development or inner blossoming.

Think, too, of the colour yellow representing the life-giving power of the sun. It is this, as well as any rain (figuratively speaking) that falls into your life, that enables that inner blossoming to take place.

6

Imagine the colour yellow suffusing this chakra as a limitless outpouring of solar energy. Picture that energy as an envelope of power not only in your mind but all around you – including under your feet where you sit. With your mind draw that power up into the solar plexus chakra just above your navel and below your rib cage, where it rotates clockwise. Picture that rotation within yourself. You have used the mandala to flood yourself with an energizing, healing tonic.

Know that this healing tonic will provide you with the strength to convert your potential into effective action. You are equipped to make any internal or external changes you deem necessary, and to respond well to any challenges that come your way.

As your gaze penetrates the root chakra symbol, imagine that the energy in your solar plexus chakra is flowering within you, in a process fuelled by your inner sun as well as the sun above. The inverted triangle is a route map for creativity. The flowering is also a blaze of passion – the "fire in your belly".

Feel creative passion filling you, and in particular giving strength to your digestive system, with which this chakra is closely connected. Relish this state of passionate engagement. When ready, take your attention back to the mandala.

"Turn your face to the sun and the shadows fall behind you."

Maori saying from New Zealand

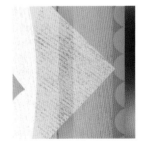

PAIN RELIEF:
BANISHING THE DEMON

Pain is an emotional as well as a physical experience. The emotional part can be diminished by meditation – after all, emotions only affect us if we allow them to. Refusing pain our permission is an art that can be learned.

Pain is not merely a response in the nerves to a trigger in the body. It is something far more complex than this: emotional factors also come into play.

In fact, it appears that what we experience as pain is partly an emotion, infused with fear. We interpret our pain, which means that the intellect also informs our response. Some of the discomfort we feel is usually stress resulting from a number of factors. One of these, if no clear diagnosis has been given, might be that we do not yet know the pain's cause: uncertainty makes us more anxious. In addition, we might not know how much longer we will need to put up with the burden. Added to these considerations, we might find the pain difficult to live with because, instead of accepting it and attempting to find space for it in our lives, we waste energy in futile resistance.

Mindfulness is a useful tool in coming to terms with pain, since concentrating fully on the moment removes two dimensions of anxiety: the past (regretting the course of events) and the future (worrying about the outcome). That does not mean, however, that you need to linger on the painful sensations as if they were a piece of music in some diabolic concert of the nerves. Better to recognize the existence of the pain, accept that you cannot wish it away by will power alone, and mentally scale down its significance. As with an emotion, pain, with practice, can be demoted – relegated to a background buzz that allows you to get on with your life.

Pain, of course, is invisible, and this is one reason it can gain such a hold upon our minds: we spend much mental energy trying to give it a graspable form. Visualization helps us apprehend our pain more clearly, and once this has been achieved we can choose, in an imagined space, where to place it. This is in part a matter of foregrounding a positive symbol, which in coming into view pushes the visual embodiment of our pain into the background.

Relaxation is key to pain relief, since tension in the muscles always heightens discomfort. The mandala meditation here will promote a more relaxed state of mind, as well as bringing about a mental re-calibration. Before you start, relax as much as possible with a few minutes of slow, measured breathing.

"The robbed that smiles, steals something from the thief."

William Shakespeare, *Othello*

Focus on your breathing / Enter a relaxed awareness / Gaze at the woman about to look at the bowl of water, at her own reflection, with her pains caged nearby / Take from her mind the idea of putting pain in its place / Look at the birds – the sensations she feels / Take the rainbow reflected in the bowl, her new-found peace, into your own mind

PAIN RELIEF MEDITATION

MOVING PAIN
TO A DIFFERENT PLACE

This meditation involves identifying with someone who has locked her pains up in cages.
They are harmless now. If she were to look at her reflection in a bowl of water,
she would see not the clouds above her, raining still, but a rainbow – the arc of her
own power to detach anxiety from her bodily sensations.

1

Sit comfortably with the Pain Relief Mandala (shown on the previous page) in front of you.

2

Clear your mind of any anxieties or preoccupations. Focus on your gentle breathing. Inhale and exhale slowly, becoming more and more relaxed with each in-breath and going deeper into awareness with each out-breath.

3

Now scan the main features of the mandala: the woman in a garden about to look down at her reflection in a stone bowl of water; the raindrops falling from clouds above; the cages nearby containing small dragons. The dragons are the pains and discomforts that have been tormenting her. But she has the equipment for reducing the harm they are causing her.

Focus on the woman at the centre of the mandala. Imagine that she is your compassionate surrogate: she endures your pain, which will be removed from her. When this happens, you will be free of pain too.

Look at the woman's head. Here lies the knowledge that her pain can be put in its place. By thought transference, move this knowledge from the woman's mind to your own mind. You become aware of your own superiority, through mind power, over any pain that comes your way.

Turn your attention to the caged dragons. Since pains are so close to us, it is easy to reach out and put them in cages in this way. Imagine that the woman has opened the cages and has gently ushered her pains (the dragons) in there. They were powerless once enticed outside her body, unable to resist her commands. In effect, they have behaved like tame animals, obedient to their owner's wishes.

Contemplate the birds flying around – these are the sensations the woman is having. She experiences them neutrally: they are detached from herself, no longer causing anxiety.

Turn your gaze to the woman's face. She is about to look at her reflection in the water in the bowl. Although it is raining, what she will see, over her head, is a rainbow. Think of this rainbow in your own mind. This is the knowledge that you can detach yourself from pain, like the woman. When you do so, you regain control of your thoughts. Your anxieties are diminished. Your pain is diminished, since pain is magnified by anxiety.

Conclude by focusing on the rainbow. You and the woman are now one person. The rainbow is the inner peace you have attained by relegating pain to its rightful place. Dwell for a few minutes within the arc of the rainbow, bathed in pure awareness and positive thinking.

"The longer we dwell on our misfortunes, the greater is their power to harm us."

Voltaire

ENERGY BOOST:
AWAKENING TO THE WORLD

Low energy levels can derive from illness, stress, poor lifestyle choices or low self-esteem.
Whatever the underlying cause, positive imagery in a mandala meditation
can help to provide a much-needed boost of mental vitality.

Any serious illness can make you feel tired, while there are minor illnesses that can leave you feeling washed out. Particular medical causes of fatigue include coeliac disease, anaemia, chronic fatigue syndrome, sleep apnoea, underactive thyroid, diabetes, glandular fever and depression. All these, if diagnosed, need professional attention, though meditation can still help as a complementary therapy.

Even without any fatiguing medical condition, it is common at times to feel listless, lacking in energy. Although this might be related to lifestyle issues (poor diet; inadequate sleep or exercise), often the root cause is largely a question of outlook. In particular, low self-esteem depletes our vitality. In extreme cases we simply can't see the point of making an effort. Meditation can help build our self-image through the power of positive imagery.

Poor posture is tiring, since it skews the spine out of alignment. Being homebound is also enervating, which is why this meditation has an unfamiliar outdoor setting. Light plays an important part of the symbolism here, because dim lighting levels reduce our vitality: lack of sunlight prompts the brain to produce more melatonin, which makes us sleepy.

Alertness can be self-fulfilling: once fully awake, we often remain so. We can all recognize this from our everyday contrast in mental states between lying in bed in the morning and being up and about. What is needed to shrug off psychological fatigue is a prompt, a call to wakefulness. This mandala, with accompanying meditation, provides such a trigger.

Wakefulness may seem an unexpected outcome of a meditation, but in fact the idea that meditators experience loosened attention is a fallacy. During practice the mind enters a state of heightened, focused awareness. The effect, after the session itself, can be to "relax" the mind in the sense of freeing it from stress. However, during the meditation, we are fully awake and energized. The meditation here has been devised to prolong this transformed mind-state as a lasting after-effect.

"Movement never lies. It is a barometer telling
the state of the soul's weather."

Martha Graham

Focus on your breathing / Enter a relaxed awareness / Meditate on the scene of productive work /
Choose a farm worker with whom to identify / Imagine the satisfactions of work well done /
Gaze at the other workers and feel a sense of common purpose / Identify with the windmill
sails turning / Draw energy from the sun

ENERGY BOOST MEDITATION

SUMMONING FRESH VITALITY

In this meditation, the power of the sun is sourced to energize mind and body.
The windmill shows the strength of an invisible force that ultimately
derives its power from the sun. A further source of inspiration in this practice is
the sense of fellow feeling with those who work for the common good.

1

Sit comfortably with the Energy Boost Mandala (shown on the previous page) in front of you.

2

Empty your mind of all anxieties and preoccupations. Focus gently on your breathing. Inhale and exhale slowly, becoming more relaxed with each in-breath and going deeper into awareness with each out-breath.

3

Now gaze at the mandala, with all its productive work on the land. Contemplate the windmill too – the sails turn automatically in the wind, and do their own work, but that too is due to human labour, ingeniously directed in an efficient machine. Turn your attention to the sun pouring energy onto this scene, and to the bees and flowers working similarly in non-human nature.

Choose one of the labourers, following your intuition, and focus on the work he or she is doing for the sake of the common good. Identify a common purpose with his person, envisaging him or her as a surrogate for the work of a different kind, whatever its nature, that you seek to have the energy to do.

Imagine your farmer working productively and happily. Feel the benefits he or she is enjoying: a sense of worthy labour, the self-respect that comes from benevolent action, pride in good workmanship. He or she is pleased to be making a contribution to a common cause. Imagine yourself having all these positive feelings after doing a similar job.

Look now at the workers with whom you did not choose to identify. They have been working alongside you, in selfless communal action. You feel a bond with those who strive alongside you in all your endeavours.

Now imagine yourself in the scene, with the sun pouring light and warmth onto you and the wind turning the windmill sails. All this energy in nature is not separate from you: you share it. Feel a sense of belonging with the dynamic weather system you inhabit: the wind, the sun, the snow, the rain.

Look at the windmill sails, turning. The wind that moves them cannot be seen, only inferred from the movement in trees and bushes. In the same way, you understand that you too have potential to be set in motion by an invisible force available to you.

Recognize the sun as the source of this much-needed energy. Conclude your meditation by fixing your gaze on the sun's disc and visualizing its powerful rays streaming into your mind and muscles. Feel fatigue dissipating as you draw strength from the most powerful force in the solar system.

"Believe you can and you're halfway there."

Theodore Roosevelt

ANXIETY RELIEF:
CALMING THE INNER SWARM

*Anxiety can chisel away at our well-being on an everyday basis, even to the point
of making us ill. A mandala meditation can help us to separate ourselves from
our worries and find a core of tranquil self-awareness within.*

We all know what it feels like when our thoughts flit restlessly around worries. Meditation can help us to calm the inner swarm – or storm – by taking us back to a simple awareness of being. This restoration of inner peace will probably not be permanent, but with repeated meditation practice it can in due course become so.

At its worst, anxiety affects our physical well-being. It can cause muscle tension, nausea, headaches, pain in the stomach, back, shoulders or throat, or even joint pain or tingling hands and feet. A meditation may be used as a quick-fix solution to give us a refreshing break from our preoccupations or, when performed regularly, as a long-term method of reducing our symptoms by adjusting our relationship with our own thoughts.

In this mandala meditation anxieties are imagined as a swarm of locusts that are shepherded out of harm's way. Visualizing this scene has the benefit of separating us from our worries.

Taking physical form in the imagination, as prompted by the mandala, the anxieties move away from our own being, where they are part of us, into an enclosed space in the outside world, where they are part of us no longer. This is a technique that can be applied to our emotions too. The underlying principle is that the impact of our anxieties and emotions can be brought within our own command. We can choose to banish or disable their effects, for a healing period that hopefully will outlast the meditation itself. They can only disturb our peace of mind if we give them permission to do so.

It can be helpful to compartmentalize anxieties before meditating. That is to say, if you recognize the sources of your anxiety, and place them in an imaginary box, beyond the reach of the meditating mind, the meditation can be more effective.

If you like, you can even write down the anxieties on slips of paper and place them in a physical box, or in a drawer.

"The greatest weapon against stress is our ability
to choose one thought over another."

William James

Focus on your breathing / Enter a relaxed awareness / Meditate on the meditating figure with anxieties, envisaged as locusts / Empathize with the figure's insight: that anxieties are merely responses, under our control / Take your mind into the pyramid's dark entrance and find deep awareness there / Usher the locusts into oblivion

ANXIETY RELIEF MEDITATION

FINDING STILLNESS

In this mandala meditation the setting is ancient Egypt. A plague of locusts
represents our commonplace anxieties. Traditional wisdom shows us that meditation,
rather than merely attempting to relax, is the way to banish them. You can lead
them by mind power to a place where they cannot harm you.

1

Sit comfortably with the Anxiety Relief Mandala (shown on the previous page) in front of you.

2

Let all concerns and anxieties drift out of your consciousness. Be aware of the rise and fall of your breathing. Inhale and exhale slowly, becoming more relaxed with each in-breath and going deeper into awareness with each out-breath.

3

Now turn your relaxed attention to the mandala. A figure is sitting in a hammock, inwardly searching for peace, under a hot sun. Below is a threat to serenity: a swarm of locusts, which threatens crops. The aim of the meditation is to shepherd these predatory insects, which represent anxieties, into the dark interior of a pyramid, where they can do no harm any more.

Gaze at the central figure in the mandala, relaxing in a hammock. The palm trees provide welcome shade from the hot sun. Think of the relaxing person as someone with anxieties, like all of us. They buzz in the mind, undermining peace. Here they have taken the form of a locust swarm, and the challenge is to silence their buzz by sending them into exile, into the pyramid.

Imagine the locusts buzzing away, intent upon causing damage to the crops – the inner harvest of calm that feeds your well-being. Identify with the person depicted in the mandala – if she can find peace, you can too.

Emphasize with the person as she tries to find a way of banishing the locusts. By turning her attention away from relaxation towards meditation, she understands that the insects are self-generated: they are responses to some of the problems she has, but they are not the actual problems. This becomes your insight too.

As you grow in your understanding of your anxieties, you see that they can cause harm only if you give them your permission. They are outside your true self, just as this scene with its anxious person, hammock and the pyramid is outside your mind.

Draw upon ancient wisdom to know how to herd the locusts into the pyramid. The secret is to meditate on the dark entrance to the pyramid. You enter this portal and find pure being here: your true self. Spend a few minutes gazing at the pyramid entrance and losing yourself in deep awareness.

Return your attention to the scene as a whole. Know that the locusts can be ushered into oblivion through the same portal. Imagine them retreating here and falling silent, leaving you in command, like a pharaoh of inner space. Think of a boat on the river of life, undertaking its voyage without the nuisance of locusts.

"Nothing external to you has any power over you."

Ralph Waldo Emerson

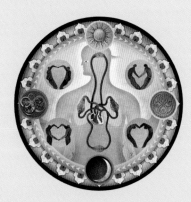

CHAPTER 4

WEBS OF LIFE

Among the natural miracles of the body are its great life-giving systems, like inner three-dimensional maps. The most obvious of these are the nervous system and the circulation of blood, both of which are the subject of mandala meditations in this chapter. Also covered here is the more esoteric traditional Chinese system of the meridians, which is the basis for acupuncture and acupressure. The chapter begins by looking at the heart chakra, centre of human connectivity.

CHAKRA MEDITATION 4

THE HEART CHAKRA

Sanskrit name: Anahata

(literally meaning "unstuck", "unhurt", "unbeaten")

Colour: Green

Element: Air

Keywords: Love, compassion, balance, serenity

The heart chakra is the source of love, compassion and joy in our life. It is located in the middle of the chest, at the level of the biological heart – balancing the world of matter with the realm of spirit. From here are woven our profound and sacred bonds with our fellow beings. The heart chakra emits a unifying force, moving us towards wholeness. Accordingly, this is a key chakra of healing. From its energy we learn to see that we are bound into the great web of relationships that spreads across the world, and indeed the cosmos.

Meditating on the Heart Chakra Mandala on the opposite page can open up the mind and spirit to such interconnectedness. As we undertake the meditation, we feel an inner expansion, enlarging our being.

Symptoms of a blocked heart chakra may include a feeling of loneliness or isolation, or sometimes resentment – an inability to find peace through forgiveness. Jealousy and being over-judgmental about other people are also suggestive of a problem in this crucially important region of the body.

SIGNS OF AN OVERACTIVE HEART CHAKRA
**Uncontrollable jealousy; grief; anger;
despair; sadness**

SIGNS OF AN UNDERACTIVE HEART CHAKRA
**Negativity; indifference; alienation;
recklessness; ennui**

THE MANDALA'S KEY ELEMENTS ARE
Twelve-petalled lotus
Interlocking triangles:
**At the intersection is a smoky area,
called a shatkona. This relates to
the union of male and female
within the self.**

"The heart has its reasons which reason knows not."

Blaise Pascal

Sit comfortably and focus on your breathing / Enter a relaxed awareness / Gaze at the mandala,
working from outside to inside via the twelve lotus petals / Think of the lotus growing from mud,
like the soul housed in the body / Focus on the heart chakra glyph with the six-pointed star /
Locate the heart chakra in the mandala, in your mind and in your body /
Feel a green light emanating from the heart chakra inside yourself, filling you with love

HEART CHAKRA MEDITATION

OPENING YOURSELF TO WHOLENESS

The heart chakra becomes so easily blocked, under pressure from competition and perpetual striving. This meditation focuses on unblocking the heart and opening up the channels of empathy and compassion. An unblocked heart gives us a better foundation for the healing of bodily ailments.

Sit comfortably with the Heart Chakra Mandala (shown on the previous page) in front of you.

Let all preoccupations and anxieties drift out of your conscious mind. Be aware of the rise and fall of your breathing. Inhale and exhale slowly, becoming more relaxed with each in-breath and going deeper into awareness with each out-breath.

Now turn your attention to the mandala. Run your gaze over the image, from the outside in. Contemplate the twelve lotus petals, arranged in two rows. Think of the symbolism of the lotus: the purity of sacred being emerging from the body, just as a beautiful lotus flower emerges from roots in the mud of a lake; and the six-pointed star representing spirit and matter coming together.

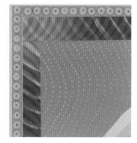

Once you have mentally progressed through the double rings of lotus petals, concentrate your gaze on the centre: the glyph that represents the heart chakra. Locate this in your own heart and consider the fact that it exists, supremely, in three places simultaneously: on the page, in your own heart, and in your mind as you do the meditation.

As your gaze rests on the six-pointed star symbolizing the unity of body and spirit, imagine at the same time that a pure green light is radiating from the heart chakra inside yourself. It is filling you with love and peace.

Don't worry if you find yourself mentally flipping between the image on the page and your own visualization of the light; if you do, remind yourself that, despite such apparent separation, all is in fact one – an integrated whole of transcendent experience.

Filling your being with glowing love, feel the green light of the heart spreading through your body. Let this sacred light radiate outwards, into the universe. You are love. You feel the power of love making you happy and mending your hurts. You know that, as your emotional hurts heal, your physical hurts are more likely to heal too.

Be aware that you exist in loving balance with all human beings and the cosmos. You need not be other than what you are. All differences – the mandala, the biological heart, the heart chakra, the feeling of infinite love – dissolve into unity. Let your consciousness divest itself of all distinctions.

Remain in this state of loving, healing being for as long as you wish. When you're ready, return your attention to the mandala on the page, using it as a bridge for your return to the everyday.

"Your task is not to seek for love, but merely to seek and find all the barriers within yourself that you have built against it."

Rumi

THE LUNGS:
BREATH'S HARD-WORKING MIRACLE

*Breath and wind have sacred connections, as we see in the idea of a divinity
breathing life and spirit into one of his subjects. At a more everyday level,
the quality of our breathing can closely reflect our state of mind.*

We carry within ourselves a portion of the outside world in the air that is captured by the lungs via breathing. The purer this air, the better it serves us. But it is also within our own gift to breathe properly, in slow, deep breaths when at rest – provided that we know how to detach ourselves from our anxieties. Breathing techniques can open a way to better health, by lowering our blood pressure, slowing a racing heart and aiding digestion.

Many languages have the same word for spirit and breath. In Sanskrit it is *prana*; in Hebrew, *ruach*; in Greek, *pneuma*; and in Latin, *spiritus*. According to Native American tradition, life begins not with conception or birth but when the newborn takes its first breath.

The mandala here draws upon an aspect of the natural world that relates to breathing: the wind, a by-product of solar energy that can be harnessed for the good, in windmills and sailing ships. Visualizing the scenario depicted, perhaps with interludes when you focus mindfully on your own relaxed breathing, will heighten in your mind the profound link between breath and consciousness. This connection is apparent from the way we breathe in different emotional states: when stressed, we take short, shallow, jerky breaths; when at peace, our breaths are long, deep and smooth.

As this mandala meditation deepens, you move closer to the source of all breath – the cosmic spirit that animates all life on Earth, via the endlessly outpouring energy of the sun.

Also important is the idea of breath as a supernatural force. In the Hebrew Bible Jehovah's breath physically and spiritually transforms the person who receives it; and Samson, having received the breath of God, tears a lion asunder. A gentler manifestation of such power is the sacred music a wind instrument can produce. The 13th-century Sufi poet Rumi wrote of the flute yearning in its soaring melodies for the reedbed it came from as the soul yearns for the divine Source.

"There is one way of breathing that is shameful and
constricted. Then, there's another way: a breath of love
that takes you all the way to infinity."

Rumi

Focus on your breathing / Enter a relaxed awareness / Contemplate the rower,
working arms and lungs / Gaze at the alveoli (air sacs, shown in the border) where oxygen exchange
takes place / Envisage the rower as the life force, keeping your breathing going /
Meditate on the red and blue alveoli / Think of the sun streaming healing power into your body

LUNGS MEDITATION

DRINKING SWEET AIR

*This mandala meditation focuses on a rower, whose tireless pumping of the oars
is imagined as the engine of your own breathing. We focus not only on the big picture
but also, at the microscopic level, on the blue and red capillaries in the alveoli
– the lungs' air sacs where oxygen exchange takes place.*

 1

Sit comfortably with the Lungs Mandala (shown on the previous page) in front of you.

2

Let all preoccupations and anxieties drift out of your mind. Be gently aware of the rise and fall of your breathing. Inhale and exhale slowly, becoming more relaxed with each in-breath and going deeper into awareness with each out-breath.

 3

Now turn to the mandala. Look at the rower, working the oars. Gaze at the clouds, birds and hot-air balloons. The capillaries in the alveoli (air sacs within the lungs, shown in the mandala's circular border) take in blood via the arteries (blue) and add oxygen (red) extracted from the air to keep the body going. This continual process of oxygen exchange underlies the rhythm of our breathing.

  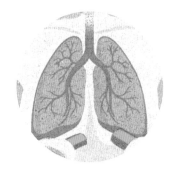

Gaze at the rower in the mandala, breathing in sweet air as she pulls the oars back and forth. This double rhythm, of rowing and breathing, is like your own double rhythm as you meditate – breathing in and out as your heart pumps away.

Focus again on your breathing as you contemplate the rower, identifying her breathing with yours. Think of her as an embodiment of the life force that is keeping your (gentler) breathing going for you. She is working hard on your behalf, so you can breathe gently, though deeply.

Feel the sweetness of the air, as the rower does. Even if you are indoors, the air is delicious with oxygen. Visualize that air passing down through your nose and into your lungs, where you can trust it to give up its oxygen for your health and well-being. Gaze at the rower's lungs as you think these thoughts.

Spend a few minutes meditating on the blue and red network of capillaries in the alveoli shown in the mandala's border. If you wish, you can repeat this unusual word to yourself as a mantra: "Alveoli, alveoli, alveoli." Like yin/yang, this is one of the basic contrasts or balances needed for life.

If you have issues with your breathing, imagine that, as well as drawing air into your lungs, you are also pulling sunlight into your head. The rower's work, as you meditate on it, is the engine for this. With each pull on the oars, more healing sunlight floods into your body, opening up your breathing a little more. The dance of blue and white in your alveoli is tirelessly benevolent.

When ready to finish your meditation, look again at the mandala as a whole, and use it as a bridge to return your thoughts to the everyday.

"What we call 'I' is just a swinging door, which moves when we inhale and when we exhale."

Shunryu Suzuki

THE HEART AND CIRCUALTION:
EMPOWERING PUMP AND PIPES

The heart pumps unstoppingly to keep us alive, providing us with an inspiring
model for compassionate love for our fellow humans. Just as a pump is a practical
instrument, there is strong practicality, too, in healing compassion.

"Great thoughts come from the heart," wrote French philosopher Blaise Pascal. In the West the heart is the seat of emotions, although many civilizations locate intellect and intuition here too. Emotion linked with thoughtfulness is a powerful combination.

As a symbol for love the heart is universally understood. Most profound is love in the sense of outgoing warmth towards others at large, not just one individual. The heart is an emblem, too, of this compassionate magnanimity.

In biology the idea of the heart as a pump is also rich in symbolism, for it suggests how important work is as an aspect of love: relationships need work, and to express compassion adequately requires us to be active on behalf of someone else – to understand their predicament, communicate generously and perform useful service.

The contribution of our time also has a part to play, since the heart never stops beating while we live, and compassion likewise is an outpouring without end.

In Islam the heart is the "throne of God", and there is something telling in this conflation of divinity with the organ that no human being can live without. There is cosmic significance also in the expansion (diastole) and contraction (systole) of the heart, a rhythm that determines cycles of time in the universe.

The mandala here incorporates all these symbolic elements, as well as the association made in ancient China between the heart and the fiery sun. One important text, the *Su Wen* ("Basic Questions"), describes how the heart "lifts itself up to the principle of light". In Sufi thinking the light of the spirit is apprehended by the "eye of the heart", and similar ideas are expressed by St Augustine.

By meditating on this mandala you can enhance your awareness of the sacred gift of life itself, understand how compassion, towards yourself and others, is fundamental to your being, and draw strength – or "take heart" as one might say in popular parlance – from these insights.

"A new heart also will I give you, and a new spirit will I put within you."

Ezekiel (36.26)

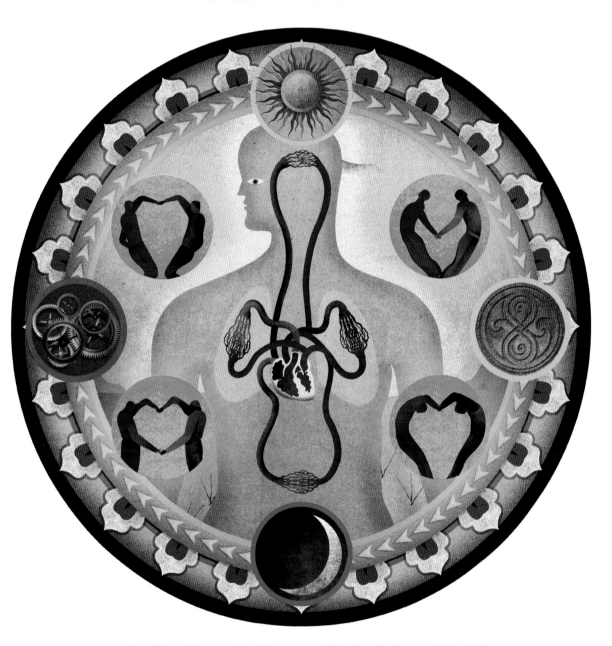

Focus on your breathing / Enter a relaxed awareness / Look at the heart and circulation pattern,
the dance of blue and red, and the time symbols / Think of the flow of blood as a dance /
Visualize the oxygen inside you as a gift, unwrapped by the lungs / Affirm that the heart is precious to you /
Meditate deeply on the circulation system, and the heart at its core

93

HEART AND CIRCULATION MEDITATION

PUMPING THE LIFE FLOW

This meditation focuses on the heart within the circulation system, pumping oxygenated (red) blood around the body and deoxygenated (blue) blood to the oxygenation chamber of the lungs. The meditation has a centring effect on heart and self. It also contains affirmations for those with medical heart issues.

1

Sit comfortably with the Heart and Circulation Mandala (shown on the previous page) in front of you.

2

Empty your mind of anxieties. Be aware of the rise and fall of your breathing. Inhale and exhale slowly, becoming more relaxed with each in-breath and going deeper into awareness with each out-breath.

3

Now consider the main features of the mandala. The central image is the heart with its circulatory system – the blood vessels that take blood to the lungs and other organs. Also shown is the dance of the heart, representing in a symbolic form as a *pas de deux*. The watch/time and sun/moon motifs underline the connection of the heartbeat with time.

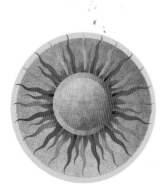

4

Contemplate the heart in its relationship with the lungs and the circulation of blood. This is a sacred diagram – a mandala – in itself, perhaps a biological version of the Tibetan mandala known as a Sri Yantra. There is no more profound image. Later in this session you will meditate deeply on this pattern.

5

Think of the flow of blood through this system as a vital dance whose magic keeps humanity alive. Turn your attention to the dancing figures, blue and red. Blue stands for the arteries; red, for the veins. The difference between them is the oxygen carried by the veins.

6

Spend a few minutes meditating on the oxygen in and around your body, invisible but all-powerful – like the life force and the spirit. Imagine this oxygen as a wrapped gift offered to you. Inside your body you remove the wrapping and use this most practical gift as the giver – nature or the divine – intended.

7

Contemplate the detail of the heart itself while making these affirmations: "I will treat my heart as precious"; "I will be true to a heart-preserving lifestyle." If you have issues with your heart, add these further affirmations: "I will honour my caregivers and show them gratitude"; "I will live my life well, whatever the limitations."

8

Gaze at the images of time within the mandala: the workings of a watch (clock time), the sun and moon (planetary time) and the symbol of time as an infinite loop (spiritual time). Meditate on each time frame in turn, progressing from the artificial to the spiritual. Know that the spiritual is the time frame of your own heartbeat.

9

Conclude your meditation by spending five minutes tracing the heart–circulation–lungs blue and red pattern with humility and reverence, starting and finishing with the heart. Use this pattern as a portal through which to enter a deep awareness of pure being.

"The heart is the perfection of the whole organism."

Aristotle

MERIDIANS:
THE WEB OF WELL-BEING

*In traditional Chinese thinking, energy flows through our bodies in a web of meridians
— lines of life force. Building on the idea of a force field, this mandala promotes
a sense of health-giving pathways within ourselves.*

We are all familiar with two vital networks within ourselves: the circulation of the blood, and the nervous system. There is a third network that is central, in ancient Chinese tradition, to our health and well-being; that is to say, the meridians.

A meridian is an "energy highway" through which *qi* (pronounced "chee") energy flows in a complex pattern of pathways. There are twelve main meridians, which travel just under the surface of the skin and penetrate into the body to connect with the organs. Each is named for the main organ, or physical system, that it governs. When energy flows correctly through this network, the person has good health; when there is a blockage, or when the energy is stagnant or weak, sickness results. It is helpful, perhaps, to think of this network as a force field, rather like a set of electric currents that flow independently of any wires.

Practitioners of Traditional Chinese Medicine know exactly how and where to access the qi energy of the body to facilitate healing, by locating and simulating acupuncture points along the meridians, to ease the energy flow. The ultimate cause of an energy blockage is traditionally perceived as a negative emotion affecting the person's behaviour — for example, leading them to poor diet.

The mandala presented here is based, not on a precise map of the meridians, but on the general principle of an energy web, envisaged as an underground network of streams linking ocean pools. The meditator imagines himself or herself on the brink of such a pool, hearing the bubbling flow of energy all around, while drawing up the life force from the earth.

The purpose of the meditation is to strengthen our sense of life energy flowing through our bodies and minds and connecting us to the cosmic, solar or divine source from which it originates. In the process we subtly gain in awareness. Two aspects of our well-being — the spiritual and physical — reinforce each other like rays of healing light from a pair of twinned stars.

"We carry within us the wonders we seek without us."

Sir Thomas Browne

Focus on your breathing / Enter a relaxed awareness / Gaze at the figure with the meridians
shown and at the underground stream-and-pool system / Feel qi (energy) flowing through your twelve
meridians, but with blockages / Imagine wading in the water: the water energy complements
earth energy / Feel the freeing of blockages

MERIDIANS MEDITATION

NETWORKING

This mandala depicts the energy lines, or meridians, within the body, but to enlarge the scale for meditation it also presents the energy system as a network of underground pools and streams. Identifying with the central figure, you imagine yourself wading into the water, which frees you of internal blockages.

1

Sit comfortably with the Meridians Mandala (shown on the previous page) in front of you.

2

Let go of any worries or preoccupations in your mind. Be gently aware of your relaxed breathing. Inhale and exhale slowly, becoming more relaxed with each in-breath and going deeper into awareness with each out-breath.

3

Now turn your attention to the mandala: the figure is shown with an approximate indication of the twelve meridians – energy lines within the body. Because it is difficult to visualize meridians individually without specialized knowledge, the energy system is also represented by a network of underground streams and pools. Imagine you are the figure, standing beside one of these pools.

You feel the life energy (qi) flowing through your twelve main meridians. Broadly speaking, it flows from the chest area along three arm yin channels to the hands. There, they connect with three arm yang channels and flow up to the head, where they connect with three leg yang channels and flow down to the feet. Here, in turn, they connect with three leg yin channels and flow up again to the chest, to complete the cycle of energy flow.

You imagine that, in places, this force is not flowing perfectly: there are blockages. Hence your visit to this place of healing.

Next, by an act of conscious will, you draw earth energy up through your feet to help with your rebalancing. Equally important is the water energy in the system of streams and pools. You imagine wading into the pool up to your knees to tap into this source of healing.

Feel your profound connection with the whole energy system. By stepping into this system, you regularize the imbalances. You feel water energy surging through you and clearing your meridians, as if you had undertaken an acupuncture session.

Imagine the meridians in your body as pipes with one or two kinks in them that are making you feel not quite wholly yourself. The water has the effect of straightening out these kinks, and making you feel more comfortable within your own self. You feel balanced again, and ready to meet any challenge. You are better equipped to deal, for example, with illness, disappointment, change or loss.

To bring your meridian meditation to an end, imagine wading through the stream out of a cave entrance onto a beach. From here you walk inland to a village – the everyday world.

"Be moderate in order to taste the joys of life in abundance."

Epicurus

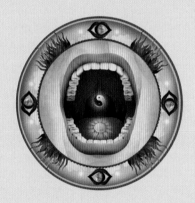

CHAPTER 5

PATHS AND GATEWAYS

Our body's systems for respiration and digestion connect ingeniously at mouth and throat. Both systems have symbolic resonance. If, above all, it is breath that lends itself to mandala meditation, this is partly because breathing operates by a conspicuous in-out rhythm; but also because breath is so closely linked, through speaking and singing, with creative self-expression. This chapter starts with the throat chakra, goes on to deal with taste and digestion and concludes on a musical note with song. By nurturing self-expression we find a meaning in our lives that is potentially a source of strength in difficult times.

CHAKRA MEDITATION 5

THE THROAT CHAKRA

Sanskrit name: Visuddha

(literally meaning "extra-pure")

Colour: Blue

Element: Water

Keywords: Truth, integrity, honesty, self-expression

The throat chakra, the first of the higher (spiritual) chakras in the chakra ladder, is the source of communication and healing. It is concerned with expressing our own original and authentic truth in our own unique way. It can be stimulated by singing.

Positioned at the neck and throat, the throat chakra enables us to gain and share accurate insights beyond extraneous factors such as time, space and social conditioning. It has the power to eradicate negative thinking through creative engagement and self-expression. It also helps us to understand the possible consequences of everything that we say or do.

Meditating on the Throat Chakra Mandala equips us to champion what we truly believe, to say no when necessary, and to be sincere and direct in our communication with others.

When this chakra is out of kilter, the health of the other chakras can be adversely affected. However, when it is in perfect balance, we express ourselves accurately, with complete honesty about what we think and feel, and we are creative and magnanimous.

SIGNS OF AN OVERACTIVE THROAT CHAKRA

Inflexible opinions; raising the voice in anger or irritation; being intolerant or critical of others

SIGNS OF AN UNDERACTIVE THROAT CHAKRA

Inability to express yourself clearly; avoidance of difficult subjects; fear of public speaking; shyness; creative blocks

THE MANDALA'S KEY ELEMENTS ARE

Sixteen lotus petals

Inverted triangle

Inner circle:

The inner circle of the mandala evokes purity and perfection.

White sphere:

This central element is the full moon, a symbol of intuitive perception.

Sit comfortably and focus on your breathing / Enter a relaxed awareness /
Gaze at the mandala: sixteen lotus petals; upward-pointing triangle; inner circle; central full moon
(intuition); glyph / Think of the lotus as the sacredness of life and the triangle as inner blossoming /
Imagine purifying blue light, rotating around your throat chakra to make you more authentic /
Feel your increased perception and power of communication

THROAT CHAKRA MEDITATION

EXPRESSING YOUR TRUE SELF

The Throat Chakra Mandala meditation is concerned with attaining a purity
of mind and feeling – the ability to perceive and communicate clearly.
This has advantages in our relationships and, if we are unwell, in our ability
to communicate effectively with our healers.

Sit comfortably with the Throat Chakra Mandala (shown on the previous page) in front of you.

Let go of all anxieties and preoccupations in your mind. Attend to the rise and fall of your breathing. Inhale and exhale slowly. Be aware of yourself becoming more relaxed with each in-breath and, with each out-breath, moving deeper into awareness.

Now turn your relaxed attention to the Throat Chakra Mandala. Run your gaze over the main features of the mandala image, starting with the outer frame and working inwards to the centre. Contemplate the sixteen lotus petals, the inner circle, and within that the downward-pointing triangle, which is symbolic of becoming. Within the triangle is a white disc that represents the full moon.

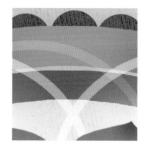

Think of the symbolism of the mandala: the lotus, as in other chakra mandalas, representing sacred life emerging out of the physical body; the inverted triangle, meaning inner blossoming; and the full moon, meaning intuition.

Think, too, of the colour blue representing clarity. It relates to the blue of the sky – the absence of clouds, meaning unobstructed communication. Think of the sky within your mind: the spaces between thoughts and feelings.

Imagine the colour blue suffusing this chakra as the colour of purity – your true nature, and the self-confidence to express it. Picture that energy, paradoxically, as a clarifying blue mist – you bathe in its power, it penetrates your skin and your body, while purifying every aspect of yourself. With your mind draw its power up into the throat, where it rotates clockwise. Picture that rotation within yourself. You have used the mandala to connect with your true nature.

Know that this new-found purity makes you feel safe enough to express yourself more honestly. You have access now to desires and feelings that were previously obscure, even to yourself – you had either suppressed them or forgotten about them, but now everything is clear.

As your gaze penetrates the glyph of this mandala, imagine that the energy in your throat chakra is enabling you to communicate great truths over great distances. The inverted triangle is a symbol of your increasing authenticity. If you have symptoms, you will be able to communicate them more effectively.

Feel the authentic self making itself at home inside you. It projects creativity and clear speaking, and both will play a part in your relationships. You now have a sharper idea of your purpose. Relish this. When ready, take your attention back to the mandala, using it as a bridge for your return to the everyday.

"The mind is what it thinks. To make it true, think true."

Nisargadatta Maharaj

THE MOUTH:
THE WORLD OF TASTE AND TRUTH

*Source of either truth or deception, depending on our attitude, the mouth
is central also to our landscape of sensation. Additionally, it relates, via speech
and song, to creativity, which can harness fiction in truth's service.*

Not counting any sensation from clothes, floor or chair, or from skin (or hair) on skin, the mouth is the only body part that can feel itself. It is the centre of feeling in the head. This makes it more important than we might expect.

Teeth and tongue are allies with contrasting characteristics. The teeth bite or chew, while the tongue does more subtle manipulation, at the same time experiencing taste. Beyond is the unseen process of ingestion and all the chemistry that follows. The mouth is the gateway to this miracle, as well as a channel for communication: symbolically it offers a combination of physical in with mental out.

At the same time, we can touch mouths, in a kiss, and with the tongue explore a part of the other with confiding intimacy; or else we can kiss with gentle affection, usually on the cheek. Kissing the hand as a token of respect has a more formal, distanced quality. A parallel with the image of divinity breathing life into the first human being gives kissing extra depth as the gift of life itself, or an enrichment of existing life.

Being a conduit for breath, speech, song and food has given the mouth overtones of creative energy, which has a role in the mandala opposite and its accompanying meditation. A significant feature is a golden solar disc placed on the tongue, symbolizing both creativity and truth. This idea is borrowed from ancient Egypt, where in a funerary ceremony a priest placed such a disc in the mouth of a deceased pharaoh to ensure that he would speak the truth when being judged in the afterlife, and therefore be granted a new life in heaven.

The point of the meditation is to promote truthfulness and dissolve self-deception, since honesty is a prerequisite of healing. The disc also denotes creativity, which in this context might mean the ability to find imaginative ways of overcoming our limitations and capitalizing on our strengths.

"Everything becomes a little different as soon as
it is spoken out loud."

Hermann Hesse

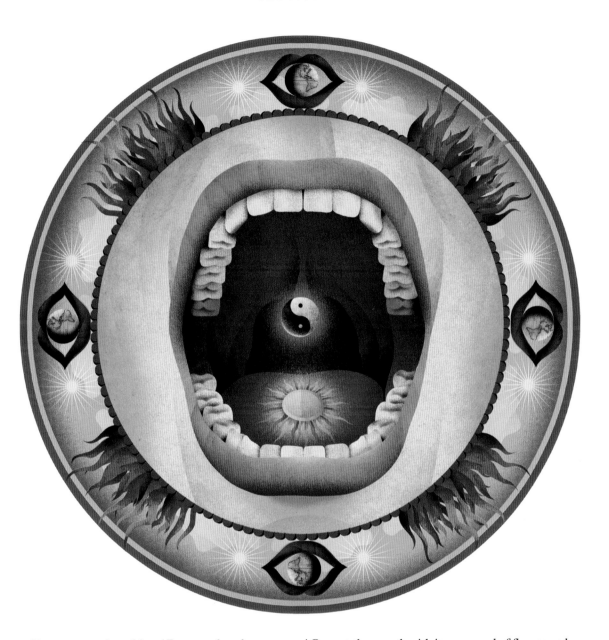

Focus on your breathing / Enter a relaxed awareness / Gaze at the mouth with its surround of flames and
world kiss symbols, its tai chi symbol on the uvula and its glowing gold coin on the tongue /
Meditate on the coin – your power for speaking truth / Mindfully attend to your mouth's sensations /
Contemplate the meaning of the tai chi symbol, flames and world kisses

MOUTH MEDITATION

SPEAKING TRUE WITH PASSION

This meditation uses the golden coin on the tongue as a symbol of sweet-tasting truth and the eloquence used to express it. It then progresses to the truth of a loving kiss – which can be no less communicative than spoken words.

1

Sit comfortably with the Mouth Mandala (shown on the previous page) in front of you.

2

Empty your mind of any anxieties or preoccupations. Be aware of your gentle breathing. Inhale and exhale slowly, becoming more relaxed with each in-breath and going deeper into awareness with each out-breath.

3

Now contemplate the mandala. Gaze at the golden coin on the tongue, symbolizing creativity and truth. This idea is derived from ancient Egypt. In funerary ceremonies a pharaoh had a golden disc placed in his mouth so he would speak the truth on judgment day and win new life in heaven. The fire around the tongue symbolizes the power of speech for good or ill.

Focus on the golden coin on the tongue depicted in the mandala. This is the ability we all have to speak the truth and use its power to effect change. Truth and creativity are not opposites: the imagination has its own truths, and imagery, as in this mandala, can reinforce reality. Imagine the coin glowing with the power of honesty and eloquence, here and in your own mouth.

Turn your attention to the sensations you have in your mouth. Move your tongue around and register the experience in your mind. Now imagine you are tasting the flavour of truth: it is sweet, despite any bitter undertones.

Feel that the glowing coin is in your mind, not on your tongue: you have moved your tongue around to push it there. You feel the power of truth filling all your thoughts. Your future communications will be clear and effective. When you speak you will express your authentic self, telling the truth as you thoughtfully see it.

Now gaze at the tai chi symbol on the uvula, denoting balance of yin and yang qualities. Consider that without balance there is no truth, since all aspects of a situation are worthy of your serious attention. That does not mean you cannot be passionate about the truth once you have discovered it.

Contemplate the flames in the mandala, symbolizing the truth passionately communicated, as well as the urgency of certain messages and of the creative impulse.

Conclude by considering the truth of love. You can kiss with the mouth as well as speak or sing with it, and a kiss has its own powerful truth, especially when it springs from pure love. The symbols at the cardinal points of this mandala are those of World Kiss Day – the globe united by the universal language of the compassionate kiss. Resolve to kiss someone with pure love on completing your meditation.

"A kiss is a secret
which takes the lips for the ear."

Edmond Rostand, *Cyrano de Bergerac*

DIGESTION:
SUSTENANCE AND ABSORPTION

The body, like the soul, needs its sustenance. The inner processing of food into energy is the physical equivalent of taking thoughts into the mind and converting them to virtuous actions.

Our digestive systems in Western cultures can all too often be a source of embarrassment: we love food but are ambivalent about the way it is processed into nutrition and waste. Such anxieties can have the effect of amplifying our stress when things go wrong with our digestion. And it's in our digestive systems – "butterflies" in the stomach – that stress of all kinds often manifests itself. Our digestion reflects our state of mind, and reminds us of the vital connections between ourselves and the world around us.

The process by which food and drink are transformed into the energy needed for life, alongside all the benefits our bodies need for efficient functioning, is a natural miracle. By meditating on that process with grateful, unembarrassed acceptance, we can prepare a solid foundation for health and well-being. By combining this with a healthy lifestyle, we enlarge our potential as human beings. At the same time, we equip ourselves, when we think about our digestion, with a resonant image of transformation: one that has endless implications for our thinking, our life projects, our problem-solving and our relationships.

In all our creative work, there will be goodness that we will need to separate from waste. We will need to be carefully selective in the first place – choosing what to consume and what to leave aside as surplus to requirements. And we will need to be patient – allowing plenty of time for adequate digestion before we gain any benefits from our efforts.

The mandala here visualizes two aspects of sustenance: the outer world of food and the inner world of digestion. The goblet and grapes stand in for the nutrients we ingest – and, of course, there is process here too, since grapes are juiced to make grape juice or transformed by fermentation into wine. The core of the image, however, is the inner maze of the gut. Two sets of symbolic associations – of digestion (transformation, filtering, enrichment) and of the labyrinth (wandering, risk, discovery) – combine to make this a resonant mandala.

"The purpose of miracles is to teach us to see the miraculous everywhere."

St Augustine of Hippo

Sit comfortably and focus on your breathing / Enter a relaxed awareness / Make acquaintance with the mandala / Gaze at the figure amidst nourishing plenty / Relish the sources of food in air, water and earth / Trace food's journey inside yourself / Visualize digestion and absorption / Attend to the mandala as a mysterious whole / Enter the portal of pure being

DIGESTION MEDITATION

TRACING THE INNER FLOW

In this mandala meditation, we start by imagining the abundance of life-giving ingredients, including water and sunlight, and partaking of a banquet of healing food and drink; then we progress to digestive function itself, tracing it both in the mandala and in our own bodies; and finally we locate a centre of truth in the labyrinth of our intestines.

1

Sit comfortably with the Digestion Mandala (shown on the previous page) in front of you.

2

Let all concerns and anxieties drift out of your consciousness. Be aware of the rise and fall of your breathing. Inhale and exhale slowly, becoming more relaxed with each in-breath and going deeper into awareness with each out-breath.

3

Now turn your relaxed attention to the mandala. Contemplate the grapes and the wine goblet, and the wheat sheaves and fishes – examples of the world's abundance. Beyond the mandala, as far as the imagination can stretch, are the world's farms, fields, gardens, orchards, seas – the rich sources of food around us. Imagine life-giving sunlight and water – gifts from the universe.

4

Gaze at the figure with arms and legs outstretched. Imagine this is you in all your potential for health and well-being. Think of yourself participating in a banquet – one of grace and moderation.

 5

Trace the journey of food both inside yourself and inside the simplified image of the mandala – it can help if you picture the mandala as a kind of scan, representing the simultaneous digestive process happening in the real world within your body. Let your thoughts flit between your real body and its graphic representation.

 6

Visualize a range of healthy foods being broken down in the stomach and then the nutrients passing into you. Bacteria in your gut are helping with the process. The nervous and circulatory systems are also playing their part. Together, a combination of nerves, hormones, bacteria, blood and the organs of the digestive system is completing the complex task of digestion.

 7

Take your eye over the whole mandala – the process of digestion and excretion – and relish this powerful image of life-giving transformations, enigmatic to you, understood by the doctors who heal you, but still mysterious at the very deepest level.

 8

Turn your gaze to the labyrinth of the small and large intestine, all coiled up in complexity. At the heart of this is the symbolic centre of the mandala: the beneficent black hole of unknowing. Pass into this and lose any sense of dualities. Within the depths of your own self you are passing into a realm of profound truth.

 9

After a few minutes of deep thought take your awareness back to the level of everyday perception. Imagine your body as a unity in which every part of the digestive process has a purpose, the whole making a complex interactive walking miracle that enables you to find and pursue your life's purpose.

"Gluttony is not a secret vice."

Orson Welles

THE THROAT AND DIAPHRAGM:
SELF AND SONG

Song is so effective a method of connecting with our own inner state that it deserves a meditation to itself. Here, larynx and diaphragm join forces to create an imaginary, mood-boosting concert for the visual and aural dimensions.

The throat has two major parts. One is the larynx (or voicebox), which protects the trachea (or windpipe) when you swallow, allows the air you breathe to reach the lungs and produces human sounds. The other is the pharynx, which leads into the oesophagus (foodpipe). The throat serves its dual purpose of air and food intake by operating a valve, the epiglottis, which closes across the windpipe to prevent any food from entering.

The diaphragm, unconnected with this system, is a partition of muscle that separates the thorax, or chest cavity, from the abdomen. By contracting it we enlarge the volume of the thorax and so inflate the lungs.

Symbolically, the throat's most potent associations are with song and speech. Song may be interpreted as the breath of the created being giving thanks for its existence. It is a more primal form of self-expression than instrumental music, since it was available before the invention of instruments, which in their different ways borrow from the physical principles behind vocal performance.

In contrast to birdsong (which is used to assert territorial rights and attract a mate), human song expresses emotions, most notably joy and sadness. Even melancholy songs convey something positive, which derives from their beauty of melody and lyric and the power of self-expression.

It is an important truth about our mind power that we can conjure up sounds and images simultaneously, just as we can enjoy both the visual and aural dimensions of an opera or music video. The mandala here uses the basic physiology of the voice as a focus for self-expression, which is a positive force even when we are singing of life's challenges. To sing, or to inhabit song in the imagination, is to assert that the spirit is indefatigable.

Singers use diaphragmatic breathing to lengthen the breath cycle and increase the volume of air they can send over the vocal cords without having to breathe in. In this meditation, however, the diaphragm is instead imagined as a drum skin adding the rhythmic beat of breath to the imagined song of joy.

"Music is the mediator between the spiritual and the sensual life."

Ludwig van Beethoven

Focus on your breathing / Enter a relaxed awareness / Meditate on the musician –
think of his drumming as your daily life, his song as your projects and relationships /
Imagine being unable to sing and other people filling the role: you still play a part in the music /
Meditate on the lyre – the beauty others bring you / In silence find pure being

PLAYING STRINGS AND DRUMS

This is essentially a meditation on the music we can make, with our saying and singing,
but also with our thoughts and feelings about others, and the things we do for them.
It is intended to be inspiring to those who, for any reason, might be unable –
hopefully just for a while – to sing for joy.

1

Sit comfortably with the Throat and Diaphragm Mandala (shown on the previous page) in front of you.

2

Dismiss all preoccupations and anxieties from your mind. Be aware of the rise and fall of your breathing. Inhale and exhale slowly, becoming more relaxed with each in-breath and going deeper into awareness with each out-breath.

3

Now turn your attention to the mandala. The tabla (hand drums) player is singing as he drums – hence the bursts of energy manifesting around his larynx. His notes appear as birds chirruping. The drums symbolize his breathing – from the diaphragm. Since song comes from the vibration of the vocal cords, this is represented in the stringed instrument – the lyre that provides the mandala with a frame.

Gaze at the central image of the musician, both drumming and singing. Imagine that the drumming is a purely physical endeavour – an unconscious rhythm, like the heartbeat. The true glory of the performance is the song, which is consciously controlled. The effect, however, is of a natural outpouring, like birdsong. Think of yourself as the song of your own life – natural and distinctive.

Spend a few minutes thinking of your everyday actions – your washing, your meals, your work, your shopping – as the drumbeat of your life, and your relationships, ideas and projects as the song. All these sounds – the sounds of a life well lived – are beautiful.

Imagine for some reason you are unable to sing for a while. You carry on drumming, but instead of singing you listen. Other people on stage with you supply their own song to your beat, and you hear this wonderful music, in which you are still playing a part.

Now gaze at the lyre, with its strings. These represent the potential beauty of life on this Earth. The notes of these subliminal strings are the good thoughts and actions that good people around you are thinking and doing. Imagine the drummer-singer is not you but someone you know, making their contribution to your well-being. The lyre plays sympathetically with this music, in your heart. You hear the lovely melody.

As you gaze at the musician, and the birds singing around him, know that the song you will sing – to the accompaniment of your heartbeat – will be true to yourself and, because of this, will move people – sometimes to joy, sometimes to tears.

Finally, imagine all sounds going silent, as you tiptoe away to an imaginary quiet room, in your own mind. Spend a few minutes in this place apart, in pure awareness of the mystery of being, before returning to the everyday.

"Truly to sing, that is a different breath."

Rainer Maria Rilke

118

CHAPTER 6

BEING AND AWARENESS

Awareness in the most commonplace understanding of the word comes from the five senses. Of these, sight has the deepest symbolic significance, giving us a metaphor for moral and intellectual perception. However, the other senses also have their nuanced associations. In this chapter smell takes us towards non-rational intuition, and hearing to sound and silence as complementary symbols of creation. The chapter concludes with a meditation on the skin, from the point of view of touch and human contact. (Taste is treated in the previous chapter, in connection with the mouth.)

CHAKRA MEDITATION 6

THE THIRD EYE CHAKRA

Sanskrit name: Ajna

(literally meaning "perceiving" or "command")

Colour: Purple

Element: Light (all elements combined)

Keywords: Perception, intuition, wisdom, illumination

The third eye chakra provides the gift of seeing – externally and internally. Its energy equips us with clear thinking, combined with self-awareness and spiritual reflection.

Seated in the forehead, between and slightly above the eyebrows, the third eye chakra enables us to grasp the outer world through seeing and the inner world through the language of symbols. It makes inner guidance available to us, piercing illusion to reveal the deep truth of the spirit. This is the chakra of mindfulness, of true awareness of enlightenment.

Meditating on the Third Eye Chakra Mandala takes us beyond the duality of good and bad to a wiser view of, for example, the body's ailments, or the complex personalities of people we know or meet. Such practice opens us also to seeing meaning in our lives – as well as helping others to gain the same insights.

Someone with a balanced third eye chakra generally has a sharp intellect with good intuition. Imbalance in this chakra can lead to a failure to find purpose in life, inability to formulate a worldview, or excessive materialism.

SIGNS OF AN OVERACTIVE THIRD EYE CHAKRA

Stress; headaches; daydreaming; mental overload; indecisiveness; poor concentration; lack of realism

SIGNS OF AN UNDERACTIVE THIRD EYE CHAKRA

Spiritual confusion; lack of empathy; unreliable intuition; memory and learning difficulties

THE MANDALA'S KEY ELEMENTS ARE

Two lotus petals

Inverted triangle

Inner circle:

Together these three elements are suggestive of profound wisdom.

Om glyph:

Om is the sacred sound of the cosmos, a hum used here as a mantra.

"I simply believe that some part of the human Self or Soul is not subject to the laws of space and time."

Carl Jung

Sit comfortably and focus on your breathing / Enter a relaxed awareness / Gaze at the mandala:
two lotus petals; inner circle; downward-pointing triangle; *om* glyph (above) /
Think of the image as the gateway to higher consciousness / Imagine purple light, rotating
around your third eye chakra to generate clear insight / Feel your enhanced wisdom /
Meditate on *om* to deepen that wisdom further

CLEARING INNER VISION

The Third Eye Chakra Mandala reflects the simple purity of true insight into the nature of existence. This meditation sharpens your perceptions, brings you self-awareness and helps you to find meaning in your life.

 1

Sit comfortably with the Third Eye Chakra Mandala (shown on previous page) in front of you.

2

Let all preoccupations and anxieties drift out of your conscious mind. Be aware of the rise and fall of your breathing. Inhale and exhale slowly, becoming more relaxed with each in-breath and going deeper into awareness with each out-breath.

 3

Now turn your relaxed attention to this simple mandala. Run your gaze over the main features: the two lotus petals, symbolizing purity of spirit; the inverted triangle, representing becoming; the circle surrounding the triangle. Consider the *om* symbol above the triangle – the mantra of grounding, focus, and recognition of the sacred. Taken together, all these elements signify wisdom.

Look at the mandala as a whole, as a gateway to higher consciousness. Its simplicity is a stripping away of inessentials. Insight becomes sharpened, facilitating self-awareness and spiritual reflection.

Consider the double symbolism of the triangle. Seen from top to bottom, its narrowing is the channelling of knowledge to the seed from which wisdom flowers – the triangle's point. But looked at from bottom to top, it symbolizes the growth and expansion of the self – the blossoming of wisdom which leads to enlightenment. Imagine this blossoming as an ongoing process within yourself.

Now turn your attention to the *om* glyph above the inverted triangle. Sanskrit in origin, this translates as "seed of all creation". Imagine it sounding as a hum in your mind, or sound it aloud, with closed lips, like a continuous mantra. This what the hum of creation, the life force, might sound like.

Imagine the purple colour of the chakra as an energy field all around you. Visualize bringing this energy up through your feet with each of your in-breaths. It travels up your legs as a purple ball of light which then passes through each of the lower chakras within your body. Finally, imagine it reaching the third eye chakra in the centre of your forehead.

With each in-breath, imagine the purple ball of energy at your third eye chakra growing larger and spinning more rapidly. With each out-breath, release any negativity associated with this chakra – for example, any confusion about life's meaning, or any difficulty in empathizing with people.

Relish your sharpened perceptiveness, which meditation has encouraged. Meditate deeply on the *om* symbol, appreciating the pure, simple truth and goodness of pure being. When ready, take your attention back to the mandala, using it as a bridge for your return to the everyday.

"Good for the body is the work of the body, good for the soul the work of the soul, and good for either the work of the other."

Henry David Thoreau

THE EYES:
LIGHT AND PERCEPTION

Although the eyes are often regarded as royal among the senses, a mandala is a visual launchpad to a non-visual experience, ultimately demonstrating that the most important truths are beyond the seen world.

The eye symbolizes perception – including the insights of wisdom. There are three kinds of eye in our understanding of life: the physical eye; the "third eye", which supplements vision with deep awareness; and the "eye of the heart", the organ of human connection.

Through the eye we receive an instant testament to beauty – provided that we direct our vision to the places where beauty is to be found (nature, the arts, the body, the spirit shining from the face). But whatever the object of our gaze, every time we look at creation we are playing our part in the miracle of perception.

If we all treat our eyes as priceless, that is because they are our gateway to the world of colour, our main aid to navigation indoors and out, and a conduit to recognition and enjoyment. Those whose visual impairments can be corrected by glasses soon get used to the inconvenience; those with partial sight struggle harder, and may need meditation to call upon reserves of courageous acceptance.

Of course, there is the mind's eye, too – our ability to conjure up an image, based on memory or pure imagination. This is a component of our empathy, our capacity for understanding what might happen or has happened to a fellow human being. In Eastern tradition we are told of the "eyes" of compassion, symbolized by the motifs in a peacock's tail. For those whose physical sight has deteriorated, the mind's eye assumes particular importance, while other senses also start to play a bigger role.

In this mandala meditation, we trace a virtuous circle of sight, both inner and outer. We start by focusing on the mechanics of visual perception, extending our awareness to the wonder of the process; then we narrow our concentration down through the pupil to the unfathomable essence behind all bodily functions; finally we lose ourselves in the eternal cosmic mystery, the wellspring of true awareness. This experience is beyond sight.

By progressing through the physical realm to the spiritual, we gain a profound sense of being at ease with ourselves and with the universe – thereby optimizing the conditions for health and well-being.

"Beauty is the soul striving to make itself visible."

T. C. Henley

Focus on your breathing / Enter a relaxed awareness / Gaze at the central eye straight
on and in cross-section, the tai chi symbols, and the images on two retinas /
Contemplate the sun, source of energy and light / Think of how our eye judges scale /
Perceive the central eye as pure pattern / Enter through the central dot into true awareness

EYES MEDITATION

SEEING DEEPER

*In this practice, we contemplate the wonder of visual perception, made possible by
the all-giving sun, but then progress to a deeper reality of pure consciousness.
We end the meditation on the black pupil of the eye, treating it as a portal
to deep and peaceful awareness of true reality.*

1

Sit comfortably with the Eyes Mandala (shown on the previous page) in front of you.

2

Empty your mind of all preoccupations and worries. Focus gently on your breathing. Inhale and exhale slowly, becoming more relaxed with each in-breath and going deeper into awareness with each out-breath.

3

Gaze at the mandala as a whole. Recognize the central eye, the flanking cross-sections of eyeballs and the images of tai chi symbols projected onto each retina, from actual symbols near the circular frame. Also, contemplate the sun, the powerful light-emitting source of energy that makes sight possible. It is presented as a flower, its rays punctuated by petals of the sacred lotus.

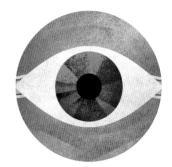

Now trace the process of vision as shown. An eye observes a tai chi symbol, showing yin/yang energy. The image passes through the lens of each eye onto the retinas, which it registers as smaller versions of reality. Think of such perception taking place as you observe these details.

Contemplate the sun in the mandala, source of light and energy. Even if you are meditating by artificial light, the sun is the ultimate energy source that makes this possible. Relish the privilege of living beneath the all-giving sun, surrounded by its revelations.

Think of scale. You judge the size of something even though the image on your retina is much smaller. Your judgment enables you to make good assessments of all you perceive. Yet when you wish to see an image as real – for example, this central eye – you can make it so imaginatively. You have the power to bring your own reality into being.

Look now at the central eye again, and strip it of its associations. See it as pure abstract image – a symmetrical geometry of form. The white of the eye becomes neutral background; the iris becomes gradations of pure colour; and the pupil becomes a black centre to the mandala as a whole – the *bindu*, as it would be traditionally called.

Meditate for a few minutes on this black dot at the centre of the mandala. You are entering deep reality through a secret passageway that takes you to pure consciousness. If other thoughts arise, let them go. When your mind is able to find a point of rest within the dot, you have accessed the ultimate truth, which is peace and love.

Once you are ready to conclude your meditation, bring your thoughts back to the mandala, and use it as a bridge to travel back to the everyday.

"No object is mysterious. The mystery is your eye."

Elizabeth Bowen

THE NOSE:
SUBTLE MESSAGES

The world of smell, lacking the orientation points that sight and hearing can fix upon, is mysterious. In entering it we lose our rational bearings and connect with primal mammalian impulses – as well as with the cosmic life force.

Like the eyes, the nose is associated with discernment. However, it operates at an intuitive rather than a rational level. Subtle smells can alter your mood, your behaviour and your choices, often without your knowing it. Obviously, humans do not have the prodigious sensitivity of certain animals – male silkworm moths can pick up a single female sex hormone, using sense receptors on their antennae, from a distance of a mile. Nevertheless, human smell tends to be underestimated. The nose is in fact a sophisticated piece of apparatus in our sensory toolkit, capable of receiving subtle messages, quite apart from the expected big signals of warning and pleasure.

Brain scans show that more of our brain is devoted to smell processing than early studies suggested. One research paper claims we can detect certain chemicals diluted in water in the ratio of less than one part per billion. This means that a swimmer could detect just a few drops of something strong-smelling in an Olympic-sized pool.

Modern science has also told us that the brain's olfactory centres are closely connected with its so-called limbic system, which modulates emotion, fear and memory.

In exercising our sense of smell we enter a world of intuitive and emotional intelligence that is far removed from the merely rational. The mandala opposite will help us enter this realm, as an antidote to the limitations of intellectual logic. What we find here is a beauty and truth beyond words.

Interestingly, the nose can identify the characteristics of a smell but not usually its source – in contrast to vision or hearing, which can pinpoint sights and sounds and convert them into a mental map. Hence, this mandala takes the meditating mind away from the visual dimension that is used initially as a prompt, into a more mysterious and profound mental ambience. In the process we connect with the spirit of the cosmos, whose phenomena are perceived as living – that is, informed by the life force – even when technically inanimate.

"Memories, imagination, old sentiments, and associations are more readily reached through the sense of smell than through any other channel."

Oliver Wendell Holmes

Focus on your breathing / Enter a relaxed awareness / Look at the mandala: nose,
sinus patterns, flowers, waves / Savour (or imagine) the scent of a candle / Imagine it sending
healing energy to you / Think of the flowers and the wave pattern as additional gifts of healing /
Meditate on a patterned circle, moving beyond the senses to pure being

NOSE MEDITATION

ASBORBING THE SCENT OF HEALTH

The following meditation, based on a mandala of the nose, can be enhanced by a scented candle, though if you prefer you can imagine the fragrance instead – a healing scent you draw through the nostrils into your whole body. The meditation ends with a journey into deep awareness, beyond the senses.

1

Sit comfortably with the Nose Mandala (shown on the previous page) in front of you, the scented candle nearby.

Let go of all worries and preoccupations. Focus on your breathing. Be aware of yourself becoming more relaxed with each in-breath and, with each out-breath, moving deeper into awareness.

3

Now look at the mandala. Either side of the nose are four patterned circles representing the sinuses – the air cavities in the cranial bones, whose function is debated: they may play a part in humidifying the air, or give resonance to the voice, or act as a buffer against damage to the face. The flowers relate to the role of the nose in smelling.

Look at the subsidiary features of the mandala too: the antennae, suggesting sensitivity, and the wave-pattern border, representing energy. Then look again at the nose. Be aware that you are observing an external body part, so obvious to others on your own face but invisible to you because of the position of the eyes. Linked with this is the nose picking up, in smelling, what is unseen. Relish the sensation of breathing, too – each in-breath and out-breath.

As you gaze at the mandala, attend also to your sense of smell. Savour the scent of the candle, and marvel that you can grasp the invisible in this way. Think of the candle as sending healing energy to you – with a confident message of hope for you to decode.

Feel this healing energy entering your nostrils and permeating your whole being through the nose's passageways, as well as via the blood vessels and nerves. You feel profoundly revitalized, and ready to face new challenges.

Turn your attention to the flowers, and think of your encounters with the scents of nature, in a garden or the countryside, as deeply healing – one of the means by which nature conveys profound benevolence: a counterpoint, perhaps, to animal predation.

Consider the wave-pattern border of the mandala, and think of this as the visual equivalent of a healing fragrance. Further healing energy enters your body through your eyes as you look at this feature.

End your session by meditating on one of the four concentric patterns that represent the sinuses – just choose any one you are drawn to. Take the pattern into your mind and imagine yourself progressing inwards through the senses towards the centre, passing through sight, then subtler touch, hearing and smell, and finally to the annihilation of all distinctions, leaving pure mental awareness – of the profound truth of being.

THE EARS:
THE ART OF ALERTNESS

The sounds our ears pick up are often discordant, but there are various hums and harmonies that carry a profound healing energy. By tuning into the primal vibration of the cosmos, we refresh body, mind and spirit.

Both sound and silence have their place in the vocabulary of spirit. Sound as music can be spiritually transforming, while in meditation a mantra – aural equivalent of a mandala – can take us deep into the truths of the self and the universe.

Within the ear is a mini-labyrinth of passageways, symbolizing the possibility that we will hear truth by a roundabout route – perhaps with false turnings. Even direct wisdom will need to be processed, through experience, before its core meaning becomes apparent. We need to filter reality from a bombardment of illusions. The ear is not selective: it is up to us, by intellectual, moral and spiritual winnowing, to sort the wheat from the chaff.

Speech, or the Word (*vak*) in ancient India, brought creation into being, using vibrations of primal sound (*nada*). Whatever we apprehend as sound is Shakti, or divine power; whatever is soundless is the First Cause. This takes us to the idea of the "primal vibration", for which the ear is a symbolic portal. Practitioners of Taoism have written of the "light of the ear". We know from experience that silence has its own hum, which derives from the body's physiology, but then that natural process is derived, like all life, from the life force. It is not so far-fetched, therefore, to contend that we can hear the primal hum of the cosmos, just by sitting in a quiet place and tuning in. Beyond this hum is the true silence, of deep space, which exists because there is no ear there to perceive it.

The mandala meditation here explores all these dimensions of sound and hearing, weaving into them the sacred Shakti symbol, which reproduces the manifestation of creation. The symbols of conches (blown as wind instruments) and bells also play a part. The practice is designed to encourage inner peace and deep perception, and to strengthen the spirit to withstand threats to well-being.

"Listen or thy tongue will keep thee deaf."

Native American proverb

Focus on your breathing / Enter a relaxed awareness / Contemplate the central Shakti symbol
and the spirals of the inner ear / See the symbol as an antenna picking up the sound of the universe /
Interpret the spirals as a template for deep thought / Imagine the conches and bells calling you /
Meditate on the central dot to find healing awareness

HEARING SUBTLE HARMONIES

This meditation centres on the symbol for Shakti, the primordial cosmic energy.
The spiral design of the inner ear is used as a template for deep thought.
You imagine the conches and bells calling you to meditate deeply and then tune into
the dot at the centre of the Shakti symbol, to find the peace of pure awareness.

1

Sit comfortably with the Ears Mandala (shown on the previous page) in front of you.

2

Empty your mind of preoccupations and anxieties. Focus gently on your breathing. Inhale and exhale slowly, becoming more relaxed with each in-breath and going deeper into awareness with each out-breath.

3

Look at the features of the mandala. The central design is the symbol of Shakti, primordial energy of the cosmos, moving through all creation like sound waves. At either side are images of the inner ear, with its labyrinth of channels – in simple terms, two ears at either side of the Shakti "nose". Gaze, too, at the conches and bells – both may be used as a call to deep communion.

4

Gaze at the Shakti symbol and imagine it as an antenna within a sounding box, picking up the deep music of the cosmos, which cannot be heard by the human ear. Your own ears may detect, in silence, a faint echo of this.

5

Close your eyes and listen: if you can hear a hum, the sound comes from your own blood-stream, but that blood flow is indebted, as all life is, to the life force. So meditate on that hum for a few minutes.

6

Open your eyes and trace the coils of the inner ear, at either side of the Shakti symbol. Think of these organs spiralling within your own body, at the appropriate place in your head. Consider the spiral as a way of travelling heal-ingly into truth, by narrowing the point of focus to exclude all inessentials. You do this when you listen to silence, and also you do it when you meditate on a dot.

7

Contemplate the conches and bells in the man-dala and imagine them all making sounds of their own accord. The conches are being blown by the breath of pure being, the bells are being shaken by the vibrations of the life force. These sounds are calling you to meditate deeply.

8

Answer that call by concentrating again on the Shakti symbol. This time you focus on the dot in the centre of the circle – the *bindu*, as it is called. The circle represents infinity, the dot represents the profoundest reality of being – in the moment, outside clock time. Meditate on the dot. Pass beyond sound and vision into pure awareness. Feel the healing energy of peace and love permeating mind and body, between which is no longer any separation.

9

Once you have completed your meditation, look in a relaxed way at the mandala, using it as a bridge to return to the everyday.

"Silence is as deep as eternity; speech, shallow as time."

Thomas Carlyle

135

THE SKIN:
OUR BRIDGE TO THE WORLD

Our skin may have shed the glow of youth, but at any age we can radiate a vitality
that transcends wrinkles. If we can shed anxiety about body image, this energy
is capable of converting inner beauty to outer attractiveness.

Technically the skin is an organ – the largest in the human body. Its self-healing properties offer an example of our superpowers: to benefit from the healing of a cut is a natural miracle, though we tend to take it for granted. The skin both separates us from others and connects us, through touch, which can make our skin tingle with pleasure or give a palpable token of reassurance.

Skin shows signs of ageing, and vanity is typically symbolized by the mirror, which some might scrutinize closely for indications of the skin's performance. To think in such terms, if it becomes habitual, may exhibit an unhealthy body-consciousness. Wisdom involves an acceptance of ageing and an understanding of its compensations – not least, a wealth of accumulated experience, including relationships. In fact, happiness has been shown to increase in our 50s and 60s, perhaps because worries about career, relationships and family have subsided. By the time we are 70 our skin might declare our approximate age to everyone we meet, but those who worry about such things have self-esteem issues and would certainly benefit from meditation to build their independence of spirit.

We may speak of youthful skin as "glowing", and there is some truth in the metaphor. However, the glow of the spirit from within is immune to time's dampening effect, and may even be enhanced in later life. It tends to show not in the skin but in sparkling eyes, in graciousness of speech, and in an irresistible vitality that can radiate through a room.

The meditation on the following pages penetrates below the skin to the unquenchable glow of the self, which permeates the whole body, whatever the perceived imperfections of ageing or illness or any other issues we might perceive. Its healing purpose is to encourage self-esteem and help the meditator value all that happens within the envelope of the skin, including the mental and spiritual connections that reach out to others and to the world at large.

"Beauty is truth's smile when she beholds
her own face in a perfect mirror."
Rabindranath Tagore

Focus on your breathing / Enter a relaxed awareness / Look at the cross-section of skin, the flower of well-being, the bridges by which skin connects us with others / Gaze at your hands: see any blemishes as badges of a life well lived / See the bridges as moments of touch – as if a healer had crossed to you / Meditate on the flower, nourished by touch

CROSSING BRIDGES

In this practice, the skin is seen as an organ – the largest in the body – but more importantly as a bridge to other people. Touch has healing qualities, even without the effort and expertise of massage. The mandala centres on the flower of well-being that is nourished by skin-to-skin touches from those you love.

1

Sit comfortably with the Skin Mandala (shown on the previous page) in front of you.

2

Clear your mind of any preoccupations and anxieties. Now focus gently on your breathing. Inhale and exhale slowly, becoming more relaxed with each in-breath and going deeper into awareness with each out-breath.

3

Gaze at the mandala as a whole. The skin is represented in cross-section, with a flower of well-being in the centre. Note the hair follicles on the upper side. There are four bridges, one at each of the cardinal points of the design – since the skin is a kind of bridge between ourselves and the outside world. Also shown are hands, the body's main conduit of touch.

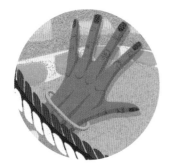

Look at the cross-section of skin, with its layers and blood vessels, and its hair follicles. This is pure mechanics. The reality we experience daily is the miracle of touch; and, according to need, the miracle of healing. Even when healing takes many weeks or even months, we have profound cause for gratitude.

Look at your hands, and think of any wrinkles, marks and blotches as badges of a life well lived. Then think of your skin as a set of clothes – washable and resilient. Your actual clothes are a kind of false skin – you might even choose to do this meditation naked, as a therapeutic exercise in self-acceptance.

Look again at the layers of skin in the mandala. You are not your skin, but neither is your largest organ, and your bridge to the world, to be undervalued – which is not the same as saying that you should worry about any blemishes or signs of ageing.

Contemplate the four bridges in the mandala. Think of four occasions when you have been touched, skin to skin – even just a handshake counts, or a pat of the hand. Think of these moments as deeply therapeutic, as if a healer had come across one of the bridges to you. As long as the bridges remain open, you have a route for healing.

Now think of all the touches you have received, skin to skin, however brief or casual, as food for the flower of the self in the centre of the mandala. Imagine this flower growing beautifully inside yourself, nourished by contact with your loved ones.

Conclude the meditation by passing through the centre of the flower into pure awareness for a few minutes. Travel deeply beyond the skin into the profound reality of being, and inhabit that simple zone for a few minutes, relaxing in peace and healing love.

"Beauty is not in the face; beauty is a light in the heart."
Khalil Gibran

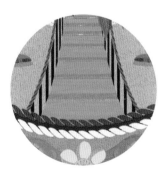

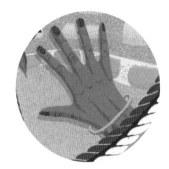

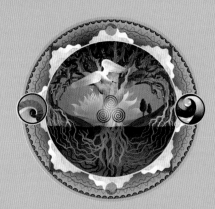

7

THE
CONSCIOUS SELF

Ironically, consciousness is both biologically and philosophically resistant to full understanding. Starting with a Crown Chakra Mandala meditation, this chapter pictures the brain's two hemispheres, connecting rational and intuitive powers, and then goes on to explore the complexities of memory and purpose. The final mandala meditation attempts to erode artificial distinctions of mind, body and spirit. Integrating all three aspects of the self into harmony through enhanced spiritual awareness gives us resilience to cope with whatever bodily ills may befall us.

CHAKRA MEDITATION 7

THE CROWN CHAKRA

Sanskrit name: Sahasrara

(literally meaning "the lotus flower of a thousand petals")

Colour: Purple / Multi-coloured / White

Element: Light (all elements combined)

Keywords: Unity, divinity, spirit, enlightenment

The crown chakra, at the top of the chakra ladder, connects us with the cosmos and the divine source of creation, enabling us to experience a mystical oneness with all other living things and even with inert matter.

Located at the crown of the head, this chakra provides us with the gift of unity through the selfless understanding that all phenomena in the cosmos are fundamentally connected with each other, in a miraculous harmony.

Lifting us high above the realm of the ego and all that can be grasped by the intellect, this chakra facilitates an experience of life's profound serenity and joy. We reach the sublime level some refer to as "Akasha" or "Zero Point Field". This is the plane where time and eternity, death and immortality, intersect.

Meditating on the Crown Chakra Mandala annihilates fear and self-doubt and releases in us a deep sense of gratitude for our blessings.

A balanced crown chakra makes us feel grounded yet spiritual. An imbalance will often lead to a lack of clear orientation in life, and a disconnection with life force energy.

SIGNS OF AN OVERACTIVE CROWN CHAKRA

Lack of common sense; feeling of superiority; inflexible sense of mission; damage to social skills

SIGNS OF AN UNDERACTIVE CROWN CHAKRA

Lack of vision or purpose; feelings of isolation, of being unloved; lack of interest in self-discovery; fear of death

THE MANDALA'S KEY ELEMENTS ARE

Thousand-petalled lotus:

Mandalas show fewer petals for practical reasons, but a thousand are visualized in the following meditation. They are purple, multi-coloured or white (a combination of all colours).

Inner circle:

In the following meditation, this is an emblem of infinity.

"God enters by a private door into each individual."

Ralph Waldo Emerson

Sit comfortably and focus on your breathing / Enter a relaxed awareness / Gaze at the mandala:
multiple ("one thousand") lotus petals ; inner circle symbolizing infinity; glyph /
Think of the lotus floating in your head and changing from purple to multi-coloured to white /
Voice an affirmation of your access to spirit / Meditate on the circle and take your mind
through it into deep awareness

CROWN CHAKRA MEDITATION

FINDING THE LIGHT OF SPIRIT

This meditation on the seventh, highest chakra, which is sometimes referred to
as the "ladder to heaven", takes you into the serenity of pure being, where the finite
and the infinite meet. The thousand-petalled lotus that features in the mandala
is a force for healing at the deepest level.

1

Sit comfortably with the Crown Chakra Mandala (shown on the previous page) in front of you.

2

Dismiss all preoccupations and anxieties from your mind. Be conscious of the rise and fall of your breathing. Inhale and exhale slowly, becoming more relaxed with each in-breath and going deeper into awareness with each out-breath.

3

Now turn your attention to the mandala, with its many-petalled lotus – think of the number of petals as one thousand, though conventionally mandalas show fewer. Contemplate the chakra which this image symbolizes as the gateway to the energy of the cosmos. It is the meeting point of the finite (body and mind) and the infinite (cosmos and spirit). The infinite is represented by the circle.

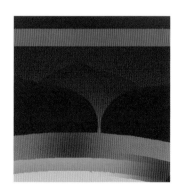

Sit with your back straight, your head held upright, and your hands in your lap, palms upward, with the left hand resting on top. This is the mudra (traditional hand position) that promotes the absorption of energy.

Gaze at the many-petalled lotus and imagine this wonderful flower coming to life and floating in your head, at the crown chakra. Visualize its petals slowly vibrating with energy. As they do so, imagine them turning from purple to multi-coloured to pure white.

Once the petals have become white in your mind, think of the differences between them dissolving into a pure spiritual light which flows down through your crown chakra into your whole being, bathing every cell of your body, every thought of your mind and every loving impulse of your spirit. You feel a deep cleansing and healing of all impurities.

Close your eyes and voice this affirmation to yourself, inwardly or aloud: "Wherever I am, the light of spirit holds me in its thousand-armed embrace." Know this light is available to you whenever you choose to access it.

Focus your mind on the intense light within yourself, and imagine that you can perceive it with all your senses. Consider it as a manifestation of a higher truth, the peace at the deep heart of being.

Open your eyes again and look at the circle within the mandala, inside the many-petalled lotus flower. Trace the endless line of the circle a few times, and then imagine yourself spiralling down into it, from time and the self to eternity and the cosmos. Feel the deep serenity of being as you travel inwards to truth. Conclude the meditation whenever you feel ready, using the mandala as a bridge to return to the everyday.

"Nowhere can anyone find a quieter or more untroubled retreat than in their own soul."

Marcus Aurelius

THE BRAIN:
TUNING OUR CONNECTIONS

The left brain is linked with intellect and logic; the right, with intuition and emotion. Often we use both sides simultaneously: so multi-faceted are the situations confronting us that a multi-faceted response is often most productive.

Consciousness is still a mystery. We know the mind enables us to be aware of the world and a person's experiences within that world, and to think and to feel. But we may never fully understand how the brain acts as host to the mind, still less the part played by personality, identity and spirit. Creation is "cleverer" than we can ever be: we have only to consider any aspect of the body's functioning, at the cellular level, to realize this.

In an age when artificial intelligence is set to transform our lives, the puzzle of consciousness raises some fascinating moral issues. At the everyday level, we might prefer to retain a traditional understanding, despite its vagueness and lack of measurable proofs. In any case, the notion of the spirit, even if many scientists may regard it as an artificial construct, is likely to be persistent, since it is so well documented by experience in many cultures over the centuries.

We rely on science for our physical and mental health, however spiritually minded we are, and there is no reason to set scientific knowledge in fierce opposition to spiritual truths, since science and spirituality are different sets of instruments measuring different aspects of the cosmos. Whether one may have insights to give to the other is a complex subject. But certainly quantum physics has been taken by many spiritual writers to confirm our intuition that some truths fall outside the reach of reason. We simply have to accept them, for the moment, without understanding why: the new science requires a leap of faith.

When we start to think about consciousness, and what we can conclude about mind from our own experience, it is easy to get tied up in mental knots. The mandala meditation here is intended to make us comfortable with what we cannot yet understand, content to take on trust the insights that intuition and spiritual faith offer us, and delighted to have at our disposal such an overwhelmingly powerful instrument as the brain.

"Think like a person of action, act like a person of thought."

Henri-Louis Bergson

Focus on your breathing / Enter a relaxed awareness / Contemplate the droplets of thought
and the ripples spreading from them / Look at the two hemispheres of the brain and the rainbow
arcing between them / Absorb healing energy from the rainbow, to empower your mind /
Meditate on the power of authentic words to help and heal

SPINNING OFF THOUGHTS

In this meditation both left and right sides of the brain – intellect and intuition – are brought into play, with a rainbow between them. You draw energy from the rainbow to tune both faculties. You conclude by celebrating the power of authentic ideas and by affirming that you will use language to help and heal.

Sit comfortably with the Brain Mandala (shown on the previous page) in front of you.

Clear your mind of any preoccupations and anxieties. Now focus gently on your breathing. Inhale and exhale slowly, becoming more relaxed with each in-breath and going deeper into awareness with each out-breath.

Gaze at the mandala. Thoughts are represented as droplets falling into water and making ripples. At either side are the brain's hemispheres: left and right. Between is a rainbow – signifying both the synapses and the revelation when one thought interacts with another to produce a beautiful idea. All around the border are winged seeds – the dissemination of thoughts around the world.

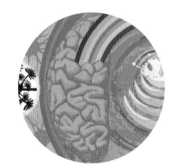

4

Contemplate the droplets of individual thought, hitting the water and spreading out in ripples. Imagine not one set of droplets but many, so that many sets of ripples interact. This is thought at its most complex. One idea reacts upon another and both are changed. Visualize this happening inside your mind as you begin this meditation.

5

Look at the two halves of the brain, left and right. Imagine you are using both logic (left brain) and intuition (right brain), and that the two are allied in a kind of mental marriage.

6

Gaze at the rainbow arcing between left brain and right brain. Think of this as a celebration of the two hemispheres working together and also as a miraculous leap of energy across a synapse – one of the junctions in the brain that enables one neuron to pass a signal to another. Connection, as in other areas of life, is everything.

7

Feel the colours of the rainbow as a source of mental power that sharpens your mind – making the logical side work more effectively and the intuitive side more wisely. Hold the rainbow in your thoughts as this recharging takes place.

8

Turn your attention to the winged seeds in the border of the mandala. These illustrate the survival of good thoughts outside your brain once you commit them to words. Think of the best things you have said – words of love, encouragement or explanation, perhaps – settling as seeds and flowering somewhere. Affirm that you will use language effectively to communicate all that is authentic in your life to help and heal others.

9

When you are ready to conclude the meditation, relax your thoughts and look again at the mandala as a whole, using it as a bridge to return to the everyday.

"The thoughts that come often unsought, and, as it were, drop into the mind, are commonly the most valuable of any we have."

John Locke

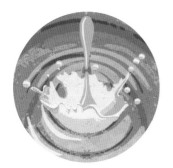 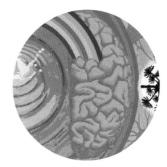 

MIND AND MEMORY:
CONSCIOUS RECALL,
CONSCIOUS PURPOSE

Memory relates to the past; purpose, to the future. Both can be sharpened in the long term by meditation. It has even been suggested that meditators may have some increased resilience against cognitive decline.

Keeping the brain active by engaging with current affairs, doing puzzles and reading thought-provoking books can help to ensure our cognitive faculties and our memory remain supple and effective, but it has been shown that meditation helps too. A 2013 study by neurologist Rebecca Erwin suggested that adults with mild cognitive impairment who practised meditation showed less atrophy in the hippocampus, part of the brain that is key in memory. It was also found that meditators had greater neural connectivity in the "default mode network", a brain system involved with daydreaming, memory and forward planning.

The mandala meditation here includes an interlude of memory, designed to liberate this faculty from habit. A habit is formed when we remember our response to a situation we have been in. Rather than responding differently next time the situation occurs (for example, behaving more confidently or optimistically), we often replicate the earlier response, simply because we expect the pattern to continue. By letting our memory rove freely over our experiences, we give it useful training.

This meditation is also devised as a way of making a firm resolve to take action. You imagine yourself pulling the levers of decision, knowing that once you have done this you will stay true to your intention. In feudal Japan it was part of the samurai code that any decision should be made within the space of seven breaths; and then, of course, that decision was regarded as irreversible. Prevarication – a habit of the unfocused mind – has no place in the meditator's mental repertoire: one is either contemplating a range of possibilities, or making a firm decision, but not skipping from one decision to another inconclusively.

Cultivating firm resolve, with the help of this meditation, has many practical applications in the context of health and well-being. For example, we might summon the will power to see a health professional, to give up a damaging lifestyle habit once and for all or to do physiotherapy in a hopeful spirit.

"Memory is the treasury and guardian of all things."

Marcus Tullius Cicero

150

Focus on your breathing / Enter a relaxed awareness / Look at the triple spiral (past, present, future),
the tree of life and the staircases of mind and memory / Place positive memories, intentions
and joys on the spiral / Imagine singing your authentic song on the tree's branches /
Ascend and descend the staircase, unique step by unique step

MIND AND MEMORY MEDITATION

KEEPING MEMORY IN MIND

*Centring on the mind's relationship with time, this mandala is in part a memory exercise,
though it also looks forward to the future and ends with an enriched experience of
the present. The moment is envisaged as birdsong, the authentic song of the
self, which may have gaps but is always uplifting.*

1

Sit comfortably with the Mind and Memory Mandala (see previous page) in front of you.

2

Clear your mind of any preoccupations and anxieties. Now focus gently on your breathing. Inhale and exhale slowly, becoming more relaxed with each in-breath and going deeper into awareness with each out-breath.

3

Gaze at the mandala as a whole. In the centre is a triple spiral time symbol suggesting past, present and future – or memory, mindfulness and hope – all going forwards, carried by a life being lived. Around this is the tree of life, its branches connecting to its roots. At either side is a spiral staircase, forming a pair – one going up, one down: these are for exercising mind and memory.

Mentally place a positive memory in the bottom left-hand spiral of the symbol and a positive intention in the bottom right-hand spiral. Then, in the upper spiral, place an aspect of your present experience that you have positive feelings about. Express to yourself your gratitude for these gifts.

Resolve to carry out your intention decisively. Stretch your memory by trying a whole range of experiences to place in turn in the "past" spiral of the time symbol. If there is something you are trying unsuccessfully to recollect, affirm to yourself that you will let the memory surface in its own time, and give thanks for it afterwards.

6

Turn your attention to the tree of life symbol, which expresses the interconnectedness of your life: the way in which the mind flits freely between past, future and present. Imagine this tree inside your mind, offering you the perfect habitat for your inner life.

Still looking at the tree, think of yourself as a bird on its branches, singing its authentic song, with clear purpose. If memory fails you at times, know that the song is still joyfully yours, and there are other birds that can be relied upon to sing what you have forgotten.

8

Turn your attention to the staircases at either side of the mandala. These are mind and memory exercises, an endless up-and-down progression, making a circle. Imagine yourself ascending and descending, step by step. The experience is different every time, since the world is so rich and the mind so supple that you can never exactly repeat yourself.

Focus on the "present" spiral of the symbol of time – the upper one of the three in the mandala's centre. Travel deeply into it with your imagination, approaching deep awareness. You are at rest with pure being. Conclude the meditation when ready, and return to the everyday.

"The past is never dead, it is not even past."

William Faulkner

BODY, MIND AND SPIRIT:
THE INTEGRATED SELF

*Body, mind and spirit, together with the emotions, are here envisaged engaging in
a dance that both promotes and celebrates the harmony of the integrated self –
in the process generating a healing energy.*

Whatever our age, we are travelling on a journey towards fulfilment – looking for ways to realize our potential, learning from our mistakes, acting in the light of our plans. Yet life is more than perpetual striving. It is what happens to us on the journey. In truth, there is no destination – other than, of course, our ultimate absorption back into the cosmos.

The journey metaphor has its limitations, as it implies a narrow track. Wandering this way and that, looking all around us, and crisscrossing the tracks of countless others, may be a more useful image. But, more accurate still, perhaps, and more inspiring, is the idea of the dance.

The mandala here features a graceful dancer, representing four dimensions of well-being: the physical, the mental, the spiritual and the emotional. The idea behind this meditation is that woman generates an energy that moves her towards integrated fulfilment – a sense of living positively, healthily and virtuously.

Dance is a language but at the same time a celebration. Hence, the meditator is encouraged to work on this mandala in a spirit of joy and thanksgiving. If there are health issues in his or her life, then thanks should be directed towards all the positive aspects of being cared for, including the love and support of friends and family, and the talents and efforts of health professionals. Since gratitude is a positive feeling, it is helpful in creating a firm foundation for the body's wounds to heal as best they can, while the inner self grows into peace and contentment, and an acceptance of life as it was, is and will be.

At a deeper level the stately dance rediscovers the primal oneness – the sense of a life cohering with all other lives, and with the cosmos itself, and finding unified purpose in existence. Body and spirit, time and eternity, the creative life force and creation itself, blend into one miraculous, harmonious whole.

"I could only believe in a God who would know how to dance."

Friedrich Nietzsche

Focus on your breathing / Enter a relaxed awareness / Imagine the dancer moving
from groundedness to spirit / Feel the symbols of enlightenment becoming weightless as you
travel deeper inwards / Meditate on the DNA inner border – your genetic inheritance /
Contemplate the doves, symbols of spirit / Meditate on the pentagram

BODY, MIND AND SPIRIT MEDITATION

FINDING WHOLENESS

*It takes commitment in meditation, as well as a pure heart, to dance above
the everyday and attain deep spiritual understanding. The symbolism of this mandala
facilitates the process. However, it is likely to work more effectively if you immerse
yourself, too, in a spiritual discipline such as Buddhism.*

1

Sit comfortably with the Body, Mind and Spirit Mandala (see previous page) in front of you.

2

Clear your mind of any preoccupations. Focus gently on your breathing. Inhale and exhale slowly, becoming more relaxed with each in-breath and going deeper into awareness with each out-breath.

3

Gaze at the mandala. In the centre is a dancer reaching up to enlightenment. Above her head are two crescent moons (mind) and a pentagram within a circle (spirit). The pentagram denotes aspiration to spiritual fulfilment. The borders have contrasting meanings: the DNA patterns suggest the physical realm, while the doves make us think of the spiritual.

Look at the double tai chi in the abdomen, which signifies the movement of the self from earth to spirit – a gradual deepening of consciousness. Imagine yourself dancing this ambitious but necessary movement as you meditate. The symbols for the four elements (air, fire, earth and water) indicate your starting point.

Turn your attention to the spiritual awakening symbolized by the crescent moons, the circle and the pentagram above the figure's head. Having balanced your complementary energies, you can now move gracefully towards an appreciation of pure being.

Imagine that your arms are lifting these symbols of enlightenment above your head, and, as you meditate towards true awareness, they become weightless: you no longer need to exert any effort to keep them aloft. Transcendence is becoming a natural function of being. Your worldly worries and preoccupations become weightless, too.

Consider the DNA pattern forming the mandala's inner border – the genetic foundation of your being. This explains why you are here now, leading the life you do. You value the genetic backstory that gave rise to your life as a dancer.

Now look at the doves in the outer border of the mandala. They symbolize love and peace. Because the doves have olive branches in their bills, following scriptural tradition, they also signify discovery. You have discovered, at the outer reaches of space, that the more mental distance you put between your circumstances and your awareness, the purer that awareness becomes. You dance in the joy of existence.

Conclude by losing yourself in the centre of the pentagram, where you become undiluted consciousness, partaking of cosmic reality. When you are ready to end your meditation, relax your thinking and use the mandala as a bridge to return to the everyday.

"Happiness is not an ideal of reason, but of imagination."
Immanuel Kant

INDEX

Main meditation entries are in **bold**

PICTURE CREDITS

With thanks to illustrators Lucy Cartwright, Anne Smith and Jesús Sotés.
Their work appears on the following pages:

Lucy Cartwright
10,14,24,31,32,33,39,40,41,42,53,54,55,57,58,58,59,64,75,76,77,82, 88,89,90, 97,98,99,
100,111,112,113,118,129,130,131,137,138,139,140,147,148,149,155,156,157

Anne Smith
7,8,17,21,24,27,28,29,42,45,46,47,64,67,68,69,82,85,86,87,100,103,104,105,118,121,
122,123,140,140,143,144,145

Jesús Sotés
10,15,24,35,36,37,42,49,50,51,61,62,63,64,71,72,73,79,80,81,82,93,94,95,100,107,108,
109,115,116,117,118,125,126,127,133,134,135,140,151,152,153

Photo Credits
Page 13: Mahesh Patil / Shutterstock
Page 18: 2light / Alamy Stock Photo

ACKNOWLEDGEMENTS

AUTHOR'S ACKNOWLEDGEMENTS
Mike Annesley wishes to thank Eddison Books, and specifically Stéphane Leduc, Nick
Eddison and Séverine Jeauneau, for having faith in this book and agreeing on the need for
top-quality artwork for the mandalas. Thanks too to Roger Walton for a design sympathetic
to the book's meaning and purpose and for spot-on artwork commissioning.

DESIGN
Roger Walton Studio

Eddison Books Limited
Creative Consultant Nick Eddison
Managing Editor Tessa Monina
Proofreader Nikky Twyman
Indexer Marie Lorimer
Designer Brazzle Atkins
Production Sarah Rooney